A Wealthy Man o₁
and Other Stories

Of course "seeing the world" changes you. Just reading about Sally Sears seeing the world practically changed me. The chapter titles alone leave you feeling windswept, and then the far-off places and the meals and the people and the animals and the good times and the sad times offer an almost-incomprehensible abundance. I have to admit I'd kind of forgotten about travel writing as a genre I enjoyed. *A Wealthy Man on the Roof of the World* has forcefully reminded me of the joys of being what used to be called "an armchair traveler." I will now gladly turn again to travel literature and intend to start right away by rereading Sally Sears's remarkable and beautiful book.

MELISSA FAY GREENE
author of National Book Award finalist *Praying for Sheetrock*

In her travel memoir, *A Wealthy Man on the Roof of the World and Other Stories,* Sally Sears dances alone down the aisle of a Russian train while singing Willie Nelson tunes. And she describes a waitress at a roadside restaurant in Australia as looking as tired as the food she serves. Making Sears the kind of traveler who returns home with stories I want to hear.

BOB PAYNE
author of *Escape Clauses*

Now more than ever, we need to be reminded of the joys of travel. Sally Sears's postcards from the past recount a marvelous expedition to such lost worlds as Soviet Russia and China in its communist heyday, making them both a delight to read and genuine historical documents. Charming, humane, and genuinely inspiring.

TONY PERROTTET
author of *Pagan Holiday* and *¡Cuba Libre!*

In 1983, just out of college, my girlfriend and I lit out with backpacks for an eight-month journey around the world, my first trip outside the USA. Europe, of course. But also more distant places: Egypt, China, the Trans-Siberian Railway via legendary Ulan Bator and Moscow. Four decades and 80 countries later, Sally Sears brought me back to those days and those places, when Beijing was a city of bicycles, the only sound on its wide boulevards the tinkling of their bells; when the Trans-Siberian was a rare ticket into the long-gone and utterly foreign world of the communist Soviet Union; when touching base with home meant tissue-thin air letters rather than email. It was solo travelers like Sears who paved the way for today's selfie-stick-toting "influencers," and *A Wealthy Man on the Roof of the World and Other Stories* is a sharply etched porthole to those days and places that made me hungry again for the smell of foreign cities and the clickety clack of long train journeys. The perfect appetizer for waiting out a pandemic.

CARL HOFFMAN
author of *Liar's Circus* and *The Last Wild Men of Borneo*

A WEALTHY MAN ON THE ROOF OF THE WORLD

AND OTHER STORIES

A WEALTHY MAN
ON THE ROOF
OF THE WORLD

AND OTHER STORIES

A TRAVEL MEMOIR BY

Sally Sears

GOOD WATER

MMXXI

Copyright © 2021 by Sally Sears
ALL RIGHTS RESERVED

ISBN 978-163732485-1

No part of this book may be reproduced in any written, electronic, recorded, or photocopied form without the written permission of the publisher, except for the use of brief quotations in an essay.

PUBLISHED BY GOOD WATER PRESS

Maps, book, and cover design
by John Balkwill, Lumino Press
Development and editing by Joan Tapper

All photographs by the author except for those
by Rob Sangster on pages 66, 77, 114, 140, and 146
and by Fred Griffith, *Memphis Commercial Appeal,* page 204.

*A Wealthy Man on the Roof of the World
and Other Stories*
First Edition

Library of Congress Cataloging – in – Publication Data
Sears, Sally 1953 –
*A Wealthy Man on the Roof of the World
and other stories* / by Sally Sears
Travel Memoir
Trans-Siberian Railroad
Post-Covid Travel
Kathmandu
Ladakh
Pacific Island Adventures
Moscow to Tahiti
Himalayas
Good Water Press

A Wealthy Man on the Roof of the World
is available from Amazon.com, Barnes & Noble.com, and
at most bookstores, through Ingram.

GoodWaterPress.com

DEDICATION

To Ralph and Marcia,
who taught us to travel.

To Steve and Randie and,
without a doubt, to Richard

CONTENTS

PART III. INTO THE PACIFIC

"Whatever you choose to do, leave tracks."
—RUTH BADER GINSBERG

PROLOGUE

A SONG CAME ON THE RADIO WHEN I WAS 28. Adventure, it promised. It teased my restless soul, telling me to see the daylight between fantasy and facts. A Jimmy Buffett tune called "Somewhere Over China" was calling to me. I wanted to see the world before I was 30, and I didn't have much time. I was already establishing myself in a career I knew would last my working life.

Television news promised a good living and interesting stories. I had started in Birmingham, moved up to Memphis, and was ready for an even bigger news town.

But I loved that Tennessee river city. The early days of increased budgets for local TV news included thrilling helicopter rides over the Mississippi delta. I covered floods in West Memphis, Arkansas, and chased Jerry Lee Lewis in a second ambulance when the first ambulance wrecked. Wrote about Elvis, barbecue, police union fights with city hall. B.B. King invited me to a quiet talk in his hotel room and was a perfect gentleman.

Still, it was a hard grind, without holidays or

sabbaticals. Meanwhile, my college classmates from Princeton were digging into professions and marriages. My roommate Eileen was even starting a family. I could see my road ahead narrowing, and I wanted a wider look before I followed it.

My parents were the first to say yes to joining me in some of the places I had to see. Dad offered to start the trip in Scotland with me so he could play a round of golf at the Old Course at St. Andrews. He was the mayor of my hometown, Montevallo, Alabama, and could only spare a week between council meetings and a mayors' convention somewhere in Arizona. Mom agreed to meet me in the Soviet Union for two weeks touring Moscow and Leningrad. Then she'd have to return to editing and publishing our family's weekly newspaper in Shelby County.

Just as I was buying my train ticket on the Trans-Siberian Railway, my boyfriend, Rob, offered to meet me in China. This was a surprise. He was a tall, good-looking businessman with a menu of interests that included lots of women. I was delighted to have his company for the far side of the world. I didn't spend too much time wondering how that would turn out.

My itinerary firmed up as I called all my Princeton buddies for recommendations. Jonny Hines had friends in Moscow and China. Ellen Porter knew USIA officials in Nepal and India. Dear George Alsobrooks, an engineer in the dark recesses of WMC-TV, wanted me to say hello to his ham radio buddy in Kathmandu. Father Moran, a Jesuit priest running a boy's school in a prime minister's palace, was the best-known ham radio operator in the world, George told me. Then maybe I'd go to Australia, New Zealand, and the South Pacific islands where Dad's American division had fought in World War II.

Meanwhile I kept hearing that song on the radio. "Somewhere Over China." I pasted the lyrics into a big red journal, and in September 1982 I took off.

Eight months later, I got a warm welcome home from everybody. What did they want to know about my trip? They wanted to hear all about it. For about five minutes. Some people were polite, some busy, some just a little jealous. So I talked a little, wrote a little, and got back to telling news stories, first in Dallas and then in Atlanta.

My journal notes spent years stashed with postcards, photos, and my letters home. COVID-19 gave me the time to sort them out, edit the notes, and remember the stories I found along the way.

MAPS

MAP FOR PARTS I AND II
ACROSS RUSSIA & AROUND ASIA

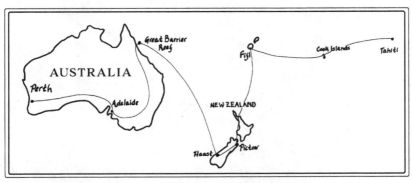

MAP FOR PART III
INTO THE PACIFIC

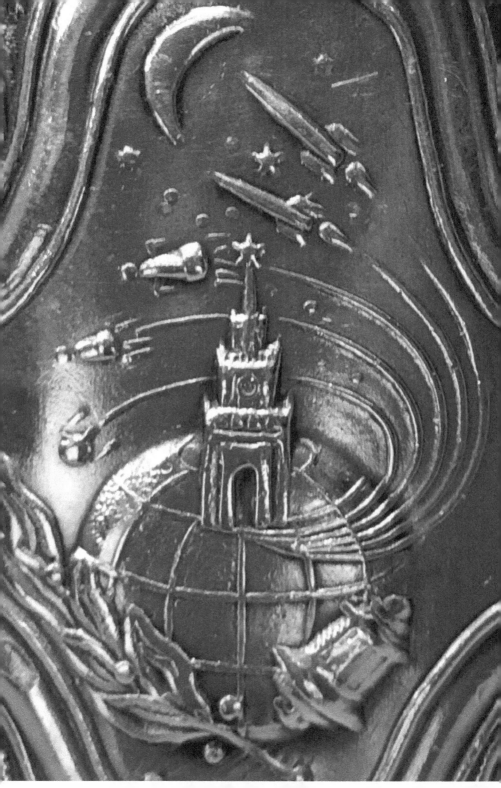

I
ACROSS RUSSIA

"Journeys are the midwives of thought."
—ALAIN DE BOTTON

THE DEEPEST LAKE
IN THE WORLD

THE TRAIN pulled out of Irkutsk and slowly climbed the hills into eastern Siberia. We left wet valleys full of birch trees and entered hills gently dusted with the first snow of the season. No roads. No people. This was the exile's Siberia.

We rounded one curve, then another. The train whipped back and forth. I pressed my nose against the window. For the first time since we left Moscow, I could see both ends of the train at once. We were running 50 miles an hour, night and day, to China. Whump! A coal train sprinted past, headed back to heat the Moscow winter.

Whoosh! A flurry of snowflakes softened the view. The train was climbing now, flakes falling faster. A genuine Siberian snowstorm blinded the trees, covering the track.

I stood in the corridor for an hour, waiting for the first glimpse of Lake Baikal, the deepest lake in the world. It was as deep as most ocean trenches, fantastically deep, more than a mile from its gray surface to the bottom. When I felt the train curve downhill, suddenly, out of the window I saw it. Baikal was a steel sliver of water, eight times as long as it was wide. Somewhere down there, invisible, the golomyanka swam.

He must be the oddest fish in the world. In water so deep, his eyes bulged like convex mirrors to catch the slightest light. He was so oily—to withstand the cold and the intense pressure of a mile of water on his back—that when the golomyanka died, he burst. The oil floated to the surface.

The Buryats, the hunters who live along the shores of Lake Baikal, scooped the oil off the surface to light their homes.

I saw a cluster of tiny homes by the railroad tracks. The train stopped, and I ran out of the station, past an astonished blue-eyed Buryat guard. It was 300 yards to the shore of the lake, and my feet flew over the rocks. I had been waiting for this run since Moscow, four days ago.

At the shore I pushed my hand between rocks into the lake. The water startled me with cold. Freezing. Cold as ice. It was rare when the water temperature reached 50 degrees on the hottest day of the year.

I searched for a shimmer of golomyanka oil in vain. The surface was dimpled only by a Russian man and his son, skipping rocks. They did not look at me. Satisfied, I walked back to the station past the dark houses. The windowsills were astonishing, deeply carved, painted red and orange, holding pots of bright flowers.

But at the train Victor, the conductor, was waiting for me.

"No good, " he said. "Trouble."

That was the extent of his English, but the message was clear. The 400 miles of Lake Baikal is or was or might be an exercise place for the Russian navy. He let me know, through an English-speaking passenger, that the guards at the Manchurian border would have to hear about my illegal run to the lake.

But until he had to turn me in at the border, he wanted us to stay friends. As if to prove the point, he brought me a cup of tea in a silver holder. He added an extra cube of sugar and smiled.

Wide white shutters on houses near Lake Baikal
focus attention on the curtains and elaborate
carvings above a well-loved blossoming plant.

Thin veins of rain lace the railcar nameplate with two scripts announcing the train's origin and destination. A bouquet of flowers in the window hints at a cozier interior world.

LEAVING MOSCOW

THE TRANS-SIBERIAN Railway was the longest train ride in the world. It ran once a week from Moscow to the Sea of Japan. I bought a ticket for the special train to China, which leaves the main track near the Mongolian border and plunges south to Beijing, the capital of the People's Republic of China.

Nine thousand kilometers, more than 6,000 miles, seven days, eight nights I would spend in a two-berth compartment, starting on a rainy Friday night. We drove through shiny Moscow streets to the train station. My young Intourist driver seemed to catch my enthusiasm. He sped up when he heard me say where I was going. "*A Chitai.*" "To China." I said, in about the only the phrase I knew in Russian.

"*Da! Da!*" "Yes, yes!"

We drove in a big circle around the west side of the Kremlin. I had a long last look at the redbrick fortress with the bright red star on top, before the Museum of Lenin blocked my view.

No Russians lingered on the streets at eight o'clock at night. We headed for the Yaroslavl station. Yaroslavl is the first town the train arrives in after it leaves Moscow. It seemed a little anticlimactic to begin the longest train ride in the world from a station named after the next stop. A bit like boarding the New York to Los Angeles express from the Rahway station. And then there the station was, big and powerful, with lots of columns in front like American train stations used to display. Nobody was in sight. The driver paid no attention to this grand building at all. He wheeled two blocks past it and then turned onto a dark muddy field. This turned out to be the collection site beside the tracks for baggage and for people.

He drove much too fast along the edge of the lot, where people were concentrating in tight bunches. Suitcases and soggy bags were piled around the passengers like wagons in a circle against the Indians. Everything—people, bags, sacks of food—all slowly melted in a steady drizzle.

By now my driver's enthusiasm outstripped mine. He wrenched my suitcase out of the trunk and galloped away to find the right track. I pulled on my orange backpack and balanced a paper bag full of groceries in my arms. Apples, butter, and a long loaf of Russian bread that poked out of the top. I felt like a stranger trying to be part of the party. I had Russian food, a soggy Russian grocery sack, blue jeans, running shoes, and standard-issue American impatience.

I drew near the very quiet crowd. Nobody looked at me. I saw Eastern faces, a big Mongolian general wearing an enormous Russian green overcoat. He looked like an extra from a movie called *Taras Bulba*. Three thin young men with broad cheekbones were laughing and talking to each other. Theirs was the only public laughter I ever heard in the Soviet Union. The driver came back. "Train is on the way," he said. Track Five. He seemed a little disappointed to leave before the train arrived. But he gently set my suitcase in the mud at my feet and drove away.

I stood by myself in a field full of Russians and North Koreans and what I learned later were 23 Swedes. No one spoke any English. Then the fifth track came alive with railroad noise. I counted 13 cars backing into the station. The Trans-Siberian, my home for the next week.

Exploring the Train

MY TRAIN CAR was magic. The compartment was bigger than I expected. One long wide berth, well padded, was covered with linen cloth during the day. Another berth folded into the thick paneling above. A table covered in white damask by the window held a bottle of flowers. Nifty little racks were everywhere. A folding ladder of polished wood led to the top berth. And, best of all, a door opened to a large sink with hot water. I would only have to share that luxury with the next compartment.

As soon as we pulled out of the station, Conductor Number Two, young Sergei with a Mohawk haircut, unlocked the toilet. I approached it with caution. Metal grating on the floor, a steel sink in the corner, raised metal footprints on each side of a two-foot-high steel toilet. I could see the railroad ties beneath me as we moved. A rack for toilet paper hung on the wall. It held a solitary sheet, the last page of a train schedule from Paris to Kiev.

Back in the compartment, I found that the Russians were strict about separating the passengers with locked connecting doors. East Germans had a car by themselves. The Russians of course were at the front of the train. I don't know where they would have put me if 23 Swedes had not been going to China at the same time. So we became the foreign car, the Westerners, the only group that got off each time the train stopped to wash the windows. It became a ritual, borrowing the conductor's stepladder and filling a bucket with hot water from the samovar. We took turns climbing up to swab at the Russian dirt that glazed the windows as soon as the train left a station. The Russians on the train with us paid no attention at all. But the folks at each station stared with curiosity.

My roommate, Martha, turned out to be a 65-year-old Swedish woman with a suitcase full of bikinis and sweaters. She seemed a little scatterbrained, with a warm heart. In Sweden she taught languages to immigrants.

Supper that first night was great fun. Martha pulled a bottle of sherry out from under the bikinis. I broke out my loaf of bread, sliced an apple, and squeezed Swedish cheese, Mildost, out of a blue tube. We toasted America and Sweden and the Soviet Union. We toasted the train for leaving on time. We toasted each others' taste in traveling companions.

Then we heard a rattle coming down the car toward us. Bottles clanked in a rack carried by a thin Russian milkman. He wore a white coat, and his teeth gleamed silver with steel. He was selling pint bottles of kefir, a cultured milk drink new to me. I bought a bottle for 35 kopecks, about 50 cents. It tasted wonderful. Sharp and smooth and thinner than yogurt, it paired well with apples and sherry. We were rich!

COGNAC FOR BREAKFAST

I WOKE UP to a gray morning and a smooth land-scape full of birch trees. We had left Yaroslavl in the middle of the night. I pulled aside the curtain when we stopped, and sure enough, that town had all the bustle of Dyersburg, Tennessee, at midnight.

Now patches of fog were creeping up to the track and falling back into the trees. Birches were every-where, miles of them, thin stemmed and white. They are a beautiful tree, with a tight fine grain. A wood-worker friend once told me 95 percent of the cabinets in new houses in America are likely to be made from white birch or its cousin red birch. He said the wood is hard, too hard to be worked by hand, and it splinters too much for housing construction. I guessed that's why so many birches were still standing along the track. I didn't think they built many cabinets in Siberia.

But even if birches were no good for building hous-es, they were terrific for my imagination. Ghostly in the fog, the trees reminded me of Anna Karenina and Dr. Zhivago. I was surrendering myself to a good spooky mood, when Sergei hammered on the compartment door and sent me to breakfast.

The restaurant car, PECTOPAH in the Cyrillic alphabet, was airy. Each table was covered in a white cloth with a cruet set clamped to the windowsill. The containers held salt, pepper, and a bunch of purple asters. Plus a menu in four languages: Russian, German, French, and English. Martha and her Swedish friends had a grim-looking breakfast of three cheese slices and more kefir. I was delighted to order fried eggs and toast. The eggs came baked, the toast was thick and black, but the waitress was smiling, and the food was fine.

I was halfway through when a middle-aged Russian in a rough coat sat down across the table from me. This contact with a Russian stranger up close was a new experience. In Leningrad and Moscow, Russians seemed to avoid mixing with strangers in public. But this man could be forgiven, perhaps because the car was almost full. "To China?" I asked him, getting a little more work out of my best Russian phrase. "*Nyet.*" No, he was going to be a worker on the B.A.M. He spelled it out for me with pride.

The Baikal-Amur Mainline was Russia's biggest construction project outside the Trans-Siberian pipeline. It's a railway that would spur off this line to the north and east of Lake Baikal, into utterly empty Siberia. I'd read the work was miserable. The earth is frozen three-fourths of the year, and in the remaining months of the swampy summer, mosquitoes wait to carry you away. Mosquito complaints are not new. Travelers writing about the hardships of moving across Siberia before the turn of the century write about wearing coats with the fur side turned inside out in the middle of the summer just to fend off mosquitoes. But the coal and mineral reserves up there are fabulous. The B.A.M. promises to deliver all that wealth to Moscow, just as this track we're riding on opened up Siberia when the last tie was laid in 1905.

I'd also read in Western papers that the project was having a hard time finding workers. I'd even heard rumors of Vietnamese impressed into service by the authorities to build the line. My breakfast companion did not seem unhappy. But he did drink half a carafe of cognac before he even started his bowl of breakfast borscht.

Mud holds an empty trailer captive in a small town where
the Trans-Siberian Railroad makes a short stop.

LEFT BEHIND
ON THE STEPPES

I STEPPED OFF the train into a brilliant Siberian morning. The air held a tang of coming cold. A smooth stroll around the train station to stretch my legs? What a good idea!

We were a dozen stops out of Moscow, crossing the Urals into the steppes, and each town was smaller than the last. But each stop lasted at least 15 minutes, so I figured I had time for a good saunter. I could easily circle that muddy plaza and be back on board, bound for China.

So off I set, wearing Brooks running shoes, a windbreaker, and an all-American attitude.

Three minutes later, on the farthest side of that nowhere town plaza, the train whistle cut the air. The engine revved. The long train began to move.

I felt my mouth open, my eyes widen. Between me and my moving train was a great vacant square of Siberian dirt. As the engines quickened, the space between me and the train expanded.

Suddenly every detail came alive.

I started to run. I felt the sun. I felt the adrenaline hit my knees, my elbows pumping.

I was going to get left behind in Ishim, the Union of Soviet Socialist Republics, with only the clothes on my back. Picking up speed, away from me, was my passport, my cash, my adventurous life as a traveler.

Oh, and trains only come through once a week.

Stranded here for a week?

Of course I ran.

On the back of the last car stood a Soviet train operator, waving a wooden stick. One end was painted green, the other red. He was facing the engine, smiling and waving the green end of the stick.

I hollered.

"Hey, Buddy!" I yelled. "Hey!"

I watched his head turn. When he saw me, the smile dropped. His eyes widened. He's leaving an American behind? Probably a spy? Certainly up to no good! I imagined him thinking his future was over.

He held out his hand and urged me to run faster. I was sprinting like a gazelle chased by a cheetah.

My feet registered the change from mud to gravel, gravel to pavement. Stretching, my fingers met his.

He pulled me onto the platform. I lay there on my stomach watching the railroad ties quicken.

Minutes later he pulled me onto my feet. Neither of us said a word, but we were both breathing hard and smiling. Then he opened the door to the last car in the train and pushed me inside.

Suddenly it got worse. The compartment was hot,

muggy, and smelled like vinegar. And I was surrounded by giants. Tall, black-haired men stared at me, dozens of them, blocking the aisle to see this exotic new creature suddenly caught in their car.

Nobody was smiling.

I didn't know the last cars on the train were filled with North Koreans.

I began to push my way up the aisle, smiling and nodding. As I got closer to the far door, I heard broken English from one of the shorter men. "American?"

I agreed.

"Why you are keeping us from our brothers?" What was he talking about? I looked at him carefully.

"Why is America forcing Koreans to be separated? Why cannot we travel to see our brothers and sisters in the south? Why is your country hurting ours?"

I had just escaped abandonment and a spy's fate in Siberia. Now I was to be a hostage to angry Koreans?

Instead I tried questions of my own.

"Who are you?" I asked him. "Where are you going? Where have you come from?"

My questions seemed to soften him. With pride, he told me they were the members of the Communist Korean Women's Volleyball Team. Victorious, coming from the Communist World Games at Zagreb, Yugoslavia!

I looked in vain for the women volleyball players. They turned out to be segregated in the next car.

Maybe it was the lingering adrenalin in my system,

but I decided to exploit the situation.

I asked if they liked communism, if socialism was working out for them, if their leader allowed conversations like this. Are only athletes allowed to leave the country? Why are the women kept in a separate car?

He, and then the rest of them, kept shaking their heads and saying it is all the fault of America.

For half an hour, one English speaker at a time, they urged, then demanded that I take up the fight for Korea against America. Why can we not be one Korea again? Why are you holding us apart?

They had never talked to anyone from the West, let alone a real American, and their sense of outrage was real.

But it was a one-sided battle. I could offer them nothing.

So I congratulated them all on a splendid athletic victory and wished them many more. We nodded together in agreement.

Finally, they let me go. I walked through both cars. The women sat on bunks, eating with chopsticks, staring at my blonde hair and running shoes.

As the train crossed the steppes of Siberia I never saw any of them at any stop along the way.

Days later in Harbin, Manchuria, the last two cars uncoupled from our train and headed down the Korean peninsula.

When the Olympics came to South Korea in 2018

I paid attention. The only participants from the North were skaters and women ice-hockey players. Perhaps their mothers or grandmothers had once played volleyball, in Zagreb, Yugoslavia.

A globe of rockets and missiles circling Red Square
reveals a worldview on a tea holder.

EATING MY WAY
ACROSS SIBERIA

THE TRANS-SIBERIAN offers a perfect week for a diet. The eating is controlled. There is no refrigerator. Naturally, I found myself constantly thinking about food. Breakfasts were invariably only bread and eggs. By the third day the choices for lunch and dinner were wearing thin.

Sadly this trip coupled my lifelong distaste for beets with the Russian national dish. Beet soup was terrible from the very first day, and by the time we passed Omsk there were no fresh vegetables at all. I noticed the Russians eating big bowls of an orange soup they called *solyanka*. It soon became a staple of mine. Heavy and beef flavored, it featured big chunks of overcooked potatoes and carrots. By now I was realizing how lucky I was to have gone shopping in Moscow with my friend Masha. A professor at Moscow University, she was a friend of a classmate of mine, and she let me see a generous slice of her life in the Soviet Union.

Masha took me to a store near Leninsky Prospekt with newspapers blocking the window. It was full of food but only for people with foreign currency. The covered windows kept less fortunate Muscovites from seeing the supplies inside. It compared to the average Russian store I'd seen in Moscow and Leningrad as Kroger does to a corner grocery. For the trip across Siberia, I had loaded up a shopping cart with a bag of hard, sour Russian apples, bell peppers, sardines, two kinds of cheese, and brown and white bread. At Masha's suggestion I added fresh yeast cakes for her mother.

The trouble with finding yeast flowed from the Soviet Union's latest effort to stem the country's epidemic of alcoholism. The government had raised the price of vodka beyond the reach of many Soviets, then found that people were using simple cooking yeast to make an evil-tasting but efficient home brew. Soon yeast cakes disappeared from store shelves. The foreign-currency store was the only place in town where Masha's mother could find yeast for baking.

At the US-manufactured cash register, the total came to six dollars. I paid for it with my American Express card. And that, too, astonished me. The Russians accepted my card and my promise to pay on my signature. While the United States and the USSR cannot agree on bombs or war, international finance can cut right through the rhetoric and make a deal for six dollars of groceries.

Before I got on the train, Masha tucked a jar of preserves into my bag. She had made them from chokecherries she'd gathered on holiday in Soviet Georgia, and they were wonderful. Her mother made a face and told me they never used to have to make preserves out of the lowly chokecherry. But now fruit was so hard to find they were preserving anything they could gather. My supplies were running low when I had tea with Swedish Martha on Tuesday. We dug into the bottom of my stash. I found a bag of pecan halves with a Piggly Wiggly price tag on the side, tiny boxes of Sun-Maid raisins, two Tetley tea bags. Eating food from home seemed enormously significant so far away.

Sergei brought us hot water for the tea bags in glasses with silver holders. Since I was in a mood to look for significance in minutiae, I studied the holder. It was elaborately decorated with grapes and leaves twisting all around the handle and sides. But when I looked closely, I saw the holder was also decorated with a globe of the world, sitting on a base of bay leaves and a space capsule. Really.

The towers of the Kremlin, with a five-pointed star on top, rose up out of the globe. A covey of capsules and rockets circled the base of the Kremlin and soared up to a crescent moon. All this ideology occupied a space I could pretty much cover with my thumb. The rockets bumped up against my nose every time I took a sip of tea. If I ever had any doubt about the Soviets' pride in getting Sputnik up first, I never again did.

SERGEI AND WILLIE

IT WAS TOO QUIET in the car late the next afternoon. The Swedes had gone to dinner, but I felt
listless and bored. I was caught up in my journal. The
books I'd brought along seemed bland. And we were
days away from Beijing.

In desperation I pulled out my cassette tape player
and switched on Willie Nelson's greatest hits, "Whis-
key River." Instantly I felt better. I was on my feet danc-
ing in the compartment, bumping into the bed. Then
I jerked open the door to the aisle and started singing
the rest of that hard-drinking headlining song

I danced down the hall, and Sergei looked up in
amazement. I turned up the volume, and he started
grinning. His feet started moving too, and we danced
side by side up and down the train car.

"Faded Love." "Momma, Don't Let Your Babies
Grow Up to Be Cowboys." On and on, Sergei moved,
his Mohawk haircut waving from side to side. He could
really dance. The Swedes came back from dinner and
watched in surprise. Their young tour guide, Maria,
danced with us, joining in a straight line in the narrow
aisle. When the tape ran out, I felt wonderful.

One of the older Swedes began to sing a folk song,

and the rest of them joined in. They pulled the older conductor, Viktor, out of his room and made him listen to their version of the "Volga Boatmen." Victor was not impressed. He threw back his head and let us hear how it *really* sounds in the land of the Volga. Deep and slow with lots of *wshhh* and *fshhhh* hissing sounds.

Then everybody else took a turn. They even made me sing "Oh! Susanna" and joined me when I got to "I come from Alabama with my banjo on my knee."

Martha passed around the last of her sherry, and we sang for hours.

After that, Sergei hounded me to play Willie Nelson again. I always did, and I always got a boost. I wish old Willie could've seen us gliding across Siberia, belting out his songs. By the time we got to China, Sergei could sing them in English.

We were great friends by then, of course. He gave me a tie tack with the train engine engraved on it. I gave him a new one dollar bill and some American postage stamps my mom had suggested as portable souvenirs. I wish I could say I gave him the Willie Nelson tape, but I did not. Music like that is too valuable to leave behind when you're 12,000 miles from home.

Why Did the Mongols Wander?

T HE TRAIN APPROACHED the Shilka River at dawn. Ice bloomed on the surface. At the river's edge the engineer faced a significant junction. To the left, along the north bank, the main line of the Trans-Siberian curves away toward Vladivostok and the Siberian port of Nakhodka. Writer Paul Theroux was quite clear about Nakhodka. He says it is a "place that gives rise to the notion that the earth is flat."

But our train did not stay on the main track. We bore right, across the Shilka, and turned south to China. Winding off to the west, I saw the slow curves of the Onon River. Genghis Khan was born on the Onon. This is nomad land. The hills are bare and old, rounded as the Pentlands in Scotland. Tiny strips of birch trees planted along the track did not look promising. It was a landscape lonely and despairing as Edward Hopper or Dorothea Lange could reveal in their art.

It was easy for me to imagine why Genghis Khan and his ancestors were called the wandering Mongol horde. I could see no good reason to settle down out here.

The shadows were sharp and short. No barbs attached to the wire fence along the track. My eye was caught by a single strand of copper, a quarter of an inch thick, shining orange in the sun. No insulation surrounded it, bright against the white porcelain knobs on a utility pole, which sat inside stacks of cross ties piled up to cow height, to protect the frail line of electricity from straying livestock.

Last night, in Ulan-Ude three Mongol horsemen rode up to the train station as we stopped. They wore big flopping hats and boots. Their faces were dark, the skin tight. One wore an animal skin, fur side in, around his shoulders. I wanted to ask them if they still drink koumiss, the liquor made from fermented mare's milk that Marco Polo loved when he came through here 600 years ago. But I didn't know the first word to say.

The men didn't greet anybody. They just stood there and watched the train. They were still watching as we pulled out of Ulan-Ude.

But I was soon reminded, despite its appearance, of the importance of this bleak corner of the earth. At Olavjannaja I saw six helicopters in the sky. They were painted the soft green and brown of desert camouflage. By now we were running close to the Kara goldfields, out of sight over the hills. In the 1800s those goldfields yielded the czar 3,600 pounds of gold a year. Now it seems the stakes are even higher. I read in a Western magazine that the Soviets have 300,000 troops and 2,000 airplanes on this border, which follows the curve of the Amur River down Manchuria toward Korea and the Sea of Japan.

This is where the Soviets are proposing to move missiles now trained on Europe. The concentration of weapons and troops reminded me how much the Soviets fear China and how intensely they guard this window on the East from so called Western powers like Japan.

Suddenly I remembered I was facing my own confrontation with the Soviets, waiting for me at the border. As the sounds of the helicopters faded, I shivered.

A bleak landscape near the border with Mongolia reveals long
train cars full of ore mined from the flattened hills.

How the Soviets
Say Goodbye

THE TRAIN STOPPED at the Chinese border about five in the evening. The Soviet border building was grand, on the same scale as the train station in Moscow. It was a powerful edifice but graceless. I was led upstairs to a small room where three solid young women were changing money. They took my rubles and handed me back wrinkled green US dollars. I unfolded each one and smoothed it in my hand, smiling down on George Washington's familiar face.

Then I waited for an hour in the cold room downstairs for permission to get back on the train. The Soviets had taken it to a roundhouse, to put new wheels on the cars so they'd fit the narrow-gauge Chinese track. They had built this line through Manchuria for the Chinese, but when the countries quarreled over communism, the Russians took up the track and the Chinese replaced it with a narrower width. This way, if either side planned to move troops toward the other, they would have to stop at the border and switch wheels.

Once, as I waited, I walked outside to get away from the heavy Russian cigarette smoke. Six guards were talking, and when I pushed open the double doors, they stiffened and moved into a straight line, their backs to me as they faced the track. I walked down the line about eight steps, and the nearest guard stamped the bottom of his rifle on the concrete. He motioned with his head for me to get back inside. I did, fast. When the train came back with new wheels, Sergei and Viktor looked stiff and unfamiliar. They wore official uniforms made of dark wool, the lapels covered with pins and medals.

My compartment looked like home by now. My Russian map was taped to the wall, with town names written in Cyrillic; my suitcase lay half open, and books sprawled across the seat. Then three Russian border guards shoved open the door and ordered me out into the hall. Two of them took the end of the bed and expertly demolished the bedding. They searched sheets and pillowcases. They ignored my suitcase and stood on the mattress to check the upper storage compartment. The third man watched me as they searched. When I stood still, he searched my papers. On my currency voucher he found my jewelry listed: one gold bracelet, earrings, one ring with 19 small sapphires. It had amazed me as I entered the Soviet Union that the customs agents had listed the jewelry. There they took my ring and counted each stone, warning me that all 19 had better leave Russia with me. Now was the time to make sure. In the dim light of the train aisle, the guard took my ring and peered at it, counting to 19 in slow Russian.

He handed my papers back, pulled out my Soviet travel visa, and stamped it. And that was another curious thing. The visa was a thin slip of onionskin paper, with a big photograph of me weighing down one end. It was my lifeline, of course, and they had demanded to see it at every hotel. Its very flimsiness doubled my nervousness that I would lose it.

The guard took it and moved down the aisle. He never mentioned my escapade at Lake Baikal. And that was it! When he took the visa, all traces of my month in the Soviet Union disappeared from my passport. It was as if I had simply levitated from Poland to China.

The heater in the car was cold by the time they left. The chill the officials left behind settled in. Then I heard a gentle knock on the compartment door. The Chinese border guards waited until I opened it, and two young women smiled at me. In slow English they asked, "Hello. How are you feeling?"

Their kindness could not have been a greater contrast to the Soviets. I knew it was deliberate, but still I melted. They asked to look at my books. One guard even leafed through one book before handing them all back.

Then they invited me to come to the office and exchange currency for renminbi, the people's currency. As we walked, I practically stumbled in disbelief at the contrast between the Soviet and Chinese handling of passengers. And inside the Chinese train station, the contrast grew even greater. A fire burned in the fireplace, thermos bottles of tea sat on tables between thick, soft armchairs. And as a final touch? Chinese babies were watching a color television. Was this the 8 p.m. day-care center for the border workers or a smooth piece of propaganda? Or both?

They fussed over me and poured me tea. One guard brought me a paperback collection of Chinese short stories. He seemed eager to practice his English. Tall, as a lot of Manchurians turned out to be, he was skinny and wore glasses. He told me he had learned English in two years, studying at home after work. So we talked a little.

He told me our train had 139 passengers. The Russians would never have given me a real number like that. He went on. Now, mid-October, was the beginning of the winter slowdown. It meant fewer passengers. In the summer 200 would pass every week, but in the middle of winter he said 60 or so border workers sometimes met just a single traveler on this train.

How had he happened to be here? I asked and then caught myself blushing. There just is not any way to make that question sound delicate. Was this posting a punishment? But he looked earnest and said it was an honor to be able to meet travelers who went through such difficulties to enter China. I wondered what difficulties he was talking about. Was this a criticism of the train or of the Soviets?

Later I was sorry I had not asked him more. He was the first Chinese person I ever talked to. I spent a month in China without having another conversation like it with a Chinese official.

As I got back on the train, I found another wonderful difference between Russia and China. The chef in the dining car had been replaced. Bean sprouts for dinner! The first fresh green thing I had been served in a week.

As I happily traded in my fork for chopsticks, I thought about the more obvious differences between the two countries. Both sides agreed this border was important. After all, the Great Wall of China had been built to keep people apart. But the Russians seemed tough in their enforcement of the separation while the Chinese seemed almost charming.

Finally I reflected that the Chinese had created their communism on a bed of Confucianism. And Confucius preached obedience to authority and respect for the good things power can bring. In a country as crowded as China, the rewards of inner control and submission have long been obvious.

In contrast, the Russians picked up their ideas of power at the end of the czar's sword. The Russian Orthodox Church certainly did not preach obedience to temporal power. Without moral reinforcement, the czars had to use more force. So it was no wonder to me that petty Russian bureaucrats at the border delighted in using power over visitors. Who else could they impress with their importance? The Chinese, on the other hand, have been in charge of themselves for a very long time. It is so clear that there was absolutely no need to rub it in.

Using a step ladder borrowed from the train conductors a passenger takes advantage of a short stop to wipe away miles of grime and better see Siberia through the windows.

II
INTO ASIA

"Struggle is the key word in Communist China."
—BARBARA TUCHMAN

Manchuria to Beijing

THE TRAIN RUSHED across the province of Manchuria. My first daylight view of the Middle Kingdom was oil wells pumping furiously outside the town of Daqing, stark against a fresh fall of snow. I'd only seen oil wells working this hard in west Texas. But this could never be mistaken for the Permian Basin.

Mud huts sat next to the oil wells. The Russians had helped the Chinese build these wells. For 10 years Russian advisers prepared the charts and tested the ground. For 10 years, nothing came up. In mid-1959 when the chill between Mao and the Soviet leaders turned to ice, the advisers went back to Moscow, taking the train track with them.

On September 26, 1959, the wells struck. The Chinese began siphoning up one of the earth's wealthiest oil fields, pumping so vigorously it was almost dry in just 20 years.

By early afternoon we were in Harbin, the northernmost Chinese city and a haven for White Russians during the 1920s. It is also a Valhalla for aging steam engines. I saw at least a dozen newly painted and returned to a life of service, each steaming at the head of a train of coal.

It was impossible to ride these tracks and miss the mineral wealth of Manchuria. Three new coal haulers sat on a flat car next to our train. They were vivid orange, the same beetle-shaped diggers with black rings around their bellies that I'd seen in the coalfields of Appalachia. And many were exactly the same. I spotted the name Island Creek Coal Company on some of the equipment.

The station in Harbin was cold and windy. We had left the warm fireplace and soft rug at the border, I realized ruefully. And no Chinese sold food to passengers as the Russians did.

As we pulled out of town we passed streets full of hay carts and crowds on bicycles. So many people! They jammed against the wooden crossing gates blocking the train tracks. In Siberia there had been no gates, nor much need for any. The few times more than one truck waited for the train to pass, the Russians sat in a careful line.

Not here! Crammed shoulder to shoulder, staring at the train windows, pointing at us, the Chinese seemed interested, full of life, pushy even. The Russian train engineer caught the enthusiasm or maybe the wisdom of a warning. For the first time all week he blew the train whistle. Often.

Then we were in Changchun, where a different legacy was evident by the side of the track. We passed a long line of tall brick towers. I assumed they held water for the steam engines. But I got a good look when we slowed down. They were watchtowers, armed by the Japanese from 1933 to 1945, when Japan occupied Manchuria as a base to conquer all of China.

Slowly the sun set off to the right. The moon was rising. It was very young, a shy little cuticle. I was glad to see it. It felt good to begin my travels in China under a new moon.

I woke up at dawn Friday after a week and a night on the train. We were pulling into the outskirts of Beijing, and I did not want to miss a minute. This was not an entrance to China prettied up for Western visitors. No trees lined the tracks. I saw squat apartment buildings, people jamming against the train guards. Bicycles thronged everywhere. The scene was vivid with movement and excitement.

At the station I saw a scene I will never forget. The station employees were exercising together on the platform. They formed ranks in their blue Mao suits and performed the graceful movements of tai chi. I marveled at the sight. It combined the grace and strength I saw in the Chinese at the border.

I pulled my suitcase behind me as I left the compartment. Suddenly it felt wrenching to leave the familiar train. I never expected it to feel like a refuge, but then it did. I waded into the masses of people at the central train station. Ahead of me there were one billion people, and I did not know a soul. I took a deep breath and walked into China.

Renting a bicycle to our foreign friend is impossible, they all said.
How wrong they were!

Renting a Flying Pigeon

THE BICYCLE RENTAL shop in Beijing was a dusty blue-painted shed across the furious traffic of Jianguomenwai Avenue from the Friendship Store. There was absolutely no reason to look twice at that place unless I was desperate to find it.

I was. After one day on my own in the capital of the People's Republic of China, I knew I had to have a bike to get around. The public buses were fine for transport, but you didn't see much of the life of the streets. On the bus I saw nothing except the backs of all the Chinese people who insisted on standing so I, their foreign friend, could have a seat.

No. For mobility in Beijing, I had to have a bike. And that's why I was searching for that dusty bike shop. My Princeton friend Jonny had told me about it. He said it was his greatest travel secret. Because in China renting bikes to foreigners was impossible. The government didn't want hordes of tourists careering through the crowded back *hutongs,* fouling up the traffic patterns. Licenses for rental bikes simply didn't exist.

But Jonny had exercised his talent for finding things that don't exist. He met an older woman with a repair shop who let him have a bike for a week. Jonny made it sound very simple. For him, it probably was. He told me the Chinese day began at sunup, so early on a Saturday morning I set out to find her. Walked down the main street of Beijing, Chang'an Avenue, until the name changed to Jianguomenwai. The Friendship Store was on the left, but because the bike traffic was so heavy, it took about five minutes to cross the street. On the other side, the south side, about half a block west toward town, I found the little blue shop of Johnny's directions.

The courtyard in front of the shop was empty, except for two men fixing a bike tire. They nodded to me, and I pushed open the door. It was dark inside. A tangle of bicycles filled the small room. Behind a rusty desk sat a tiny woman in a Mao suit. I asked her in slow English if I could rent a bicycle. She looked surprised and shook her head. I tried again, pantomiming riding and pointing to myself. Slowly she seemed to make up her mind. She stood up and nodded.

She pulled a bicycle for me out of the pile in front of us. She squeezed the tires and rang the handbell. It gave a high ring. It was a thrilling sound. Then the woman held out her hand. I was not sure how much the rental fee was, so I offered her 10 yuan in the special tourist currency that foreigners had to use in China. But no. She shook her head. She said something. It sounded like the word "passport."

It *was* passport. I handed mine to her, and she took a long look at the photograph inside. Apparently satisfied, she casually threw it behind her into an open drawer in a dusty filing cabinet.

I was nervous. No, I was terrified. But that turned out to be the deposit. I supposed a passport was a substitute for a bicycle license, perhaps the only way the woman could justify letting foreigners have a bike. I needn't have worried.

When I brought the bike back a week later, my passport lay in exactly the same place in the open drawer, wearing its own light coating of dust. Outside we pumped up the tires. And there I was, in possession of a black Flying Pigeon brand bicycle with one bell, one hand brake, one curious circular lock on the back wheel, and one speed. My own.

The bicycle was exactly the same as the hundreds of thousands of others that were speeding past the Friendship Store. I waved goodbye to the woman who had come outside to see me off and joined the crowd.

Graceful as a resting serpent,
the Great Wall of China lies easily on the hillside.
Centuries of visitors have softened the sharp stone steps.

WHAT COLOR
IS CHINESE RED?

I MET ROB AT THE end of a long tree-lined road to the Beijing airport. Both of us were amazed that despite the hazards of traveling to the other side of the world from two different directions we had connected exactly as we planned.

Lone tourists were a complication China had not yet welcomed in 1982. I heard many news reporters still calling the People's Republic "Red China" long after President Richard Nixon opened up the country to Western money and travelers. To travel to Xi'an, Shanghai, Huangzhou, Guilin, and Guangzhou, Rob and I joined a small tour group.

Right away differences in culture and translation stood out. The color they call Chinese red looked to me more like orange. A tangerine turned out to be a mandarin orange. The Giant Wild Goose Pavilion. The Peak That Flew Here from Afar. The Chinese gift for naming places and events held me captivated as we started in the heart of Beijing.

Tiananmen Square was a buzzing hive of traffic circling the vast space where Mao Zedong proclaimed the founding of the People's Republic of China. Smooth paving. No trees. No benches. Nobody. A furious surge of bicycle traffic around the far-flung edges of the famous square seemed like molecules of atoms zooming around an empty core.

On the south side of the square lay Mao himself. Despite his desire to be cremated, six years after his death in 1976 his body lay in eternal repose under the sign of a communist hammer and sickle, face waxy, sallow, and soft. That distinctive mole on his chin sank into his skin. He wore a gray Mao jacket. I could not take my eyes off what was left of this world-changing tyrant, author of the Great Leap Forward, starver of tens of millions of Chinese people.

I could not help but compare him to the last corpse I'd seen. Mao looked a lot worse than Vladimir Lenin, who had died in 1924. Just weeks earlier I'd seen the Soviet leader's carefully preserved body lying in a red room in Moscow's Red Square. Devil beard and mustache, creepy fingers, Lenin looked to me as if he could sit up and order death to dissenters all over again. In contrast, Mao looked defeated. The competition I'd noticed at the border between these communist countries now included how best to mummify leaders for public display. The sight of Mao was proof Russia won the treatment-of-dead-revered-leaders contest.

Outside of the mausoleum to Mao, on the right or, as they called it, the "East is Red" side of Tiananmen, stood the Museum of the Revolution.

Again, as in the public square itself, nobody was around. I wondered if we were even supposed to be here, in a museum barely prepared to crack open to outsiders some darker secrets of this long-closed world.

No English signs explained the photographs or cartoons or the scaffold where Chinese opponents to Mao were hanged.

I recognized a map and tattered shreds of clothing and gloves from the Long March, the 6,000-mile retreat from the Chinese Nationalists that made Mao the undisputed leader of the Chinese Communists. The bloody fabric scraps reminded me of the dozens of museums in the Confederate South still consecrating The Lost Cause. I didn't think I needed to see another stretcher stained with blood that was said to have carried some hero of a long-forgotten battle, in China or in Tennessee.

By the wall of a far room stood a black box, eight feet tall. It was the radio transmitter Mao had used to keep up the spirits of his soldiers. In the dusty silence of the museum I imagined hearing the tinny sounds of voices from beyond the mountains. I looked closely at the aging blue vacuum tubes, copper coils, and the brass nameplate. It read RCA, Camden, New Jersey. So big, yet so fragile, so crucial to Mao's winning the war. Maybe it was simply the English letters, the American manufacturing that made me feel strangely warmer toward the Chinese.

The next room cooled my thoughts. A long banner hanging from the ceiling stretched for 40 feet. It was tea colored with age, its message still ominous. Fading red Chinese characters and then English letters said, "Get Out China or China will Kick You Out, American GI."

I stood up straight and was suddenly glad to be absolutely alone. In my hands I twisted the green People's Liberation Army hat I'd bought as a souvenir and looked over my shoulder. Old enemies die hard, I realized. Old enemies do not forget.

Suddenly my mind jumped back to a childhood trip to the Panama Canal. Mom and Dad drove us down the Central American isthmus in the early 1960s. We were warmly welcomed in Tegucigalpa, in San Jose, in one capital after another. But when we arrived in Panama City, we found graffiti scrawled on a wall: Yanqui Go Home.

Here in China was another reminder of critical ideas about America's place in the world, of America as an enemy. I pulled myself out of the museum and watched bicycles spin past me.

A Nightcap at the Jin Jiang Club

EATING WAS A TREAT in every part of China. But I suffered a few migraine headaches. Now this was not a new malady. News reporting and its pressures gave me plenty of migraines. I was familiar with that side-of-the-head stabbing and sudden nausea often caused by stress and bright lights. Medicines sometimes worked. But avoiding the triggers seemed like a better solution, I thought. Could I catch a migraine break in China? Well, no.

My first Chinese migraine came with a glass of Chinese wine at dinner followed by a glass of Chinese scotch. My second? Probably caused by two weeks of eating pickled cabbage and salt. But the cause of my third migraine was in no doubt. I honestly blamed the ghost of the Jin Jiang Club on The Bund in the old European Concession in Shanghai, where the musicians played what must be the last 1940s jazz in China.

The floor was acres of deep red carpet, the paneled walls enclosed 21 linen-draped tables. Only four tables supported sleepy-eyed Chinese guests and their cocktails. And Rob and me. The Jin Jiang Quartet played "Not Too Young at All," which they definitely were. The piano and electric guitar quieted. The trumpet and saxophone lingered on the last notes. A gentle wordless pause, and then, with a nod the quartet played a dozen more songs. They'd clearly been playing together for years, these Chinese men. I watched the sharp creases in their faces, their fingers careful and quick.

The atmosphere recreated a world of martinis and cigarette holders. How it survived Mao's Revolution, let alone all the leaps forward since his death, was a mystery to me that night. So was the scotch. It may have been made in China, too. At last, the trumpet player let the saxophone carry the melody of "Auld Lang Syne" a third of an octave higher. We left transported.

The morning hangover was brutal.

I only got out of bed because the group tour that morning included the July the First People's Commune. Who would want to miss seeing a factory where they made machines? Machines that chopped metal apart. Without finger guards, I noticed.

After the tour we heard what the guide called the brief introduction by A Responsible Person. That was really her title, and she explained that the unfortunate accidents of severed fingers gave commune doctors plenty of practice and nationally acknowledged skill in reconnecting body parts.

I could only handle the first 15 minutes of her Responsible Person talk, since I was not feeling responsible at all. I left looking for a place to bury my head.

That's how I found the commune clinic and a doctor eager to rid my headache with her skills in acupressure. She held on tight to my temple and the soft spot between my thumb and first finger for 10 minutes. I closed my eyes and with each breath felt my headache begin to ease.

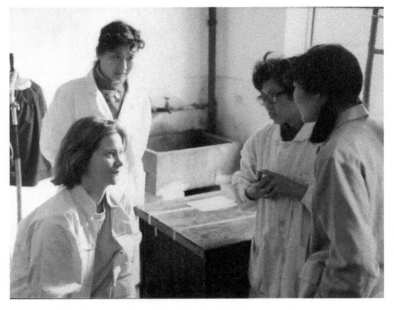

The doctor's office at the July the First People's Commune was a bare room with a sink and a single faucet.

I did not see her pick up two thin needles. I had not signed up for acupuncture. But before I could resist and ask if she'd sterilized them in Betadyne, or even the prior evening's scotch, she slid them into my temple.

I heard them crunch through my hair and skin and felt only warm relief.

She left them in for barely a second or two. Because, she told me through the guide and other group members who'd joined us, that she thought I would faint.

My left hand was numb, both hands were cold, my fainting felt imminent. But my headache was gone!

I was the daring darling of the tour.

Swanning About Thailand

IN THE LOBBY of the Swan Hotel, next to the famous Oriental Hotel in Bangkok, I spotted a sign in English. It was a relief, after leaving China, to read English letters again.

"This pool is reserved for Hotel Guest and spouse only, it read." Seemed a little odd.

I put on a bathing suit and went for a swim.

As I climbed into the water, a British woman on a deck chair watched me intently. I recalled the sign and asked her what she thought it meant. She shook her head from side to side and told me about the sex-and-sin city bus tours of Japanese men.

"They drive up to the Swan in the evening, ravening for Thai women. They check into the hotel…"

I loved her word "ravening." I asked, "In the very shadow of the Oriental Hotel?" She laughed out loud this time. "Of course! The Oriental? Lots of buses there, too."

In our hotel, the Swan, a less expensive hotel, they had many guests. Not so many from Japan but lots of Pakistanis looking for a night away from Uncle Zia.

Just as she said that, I looked up and was amazed to

see three men who looked like Pakistanis appear on a balcony on the third floor. They seemed to be leering down at us.

"That" she said, "is the reason the hotel pool is for registered guests only. Diseases."

Whoa! Then I remembered the advertisement in the tourist newspapers for venereal disease clinics.

"The hotel tries to keep the girls out of the pool..." As soon as she started that sentence, I leaped out and covered myself with a towel. The men were still leering.

WELCOME TO INDIA

IMADE A MISTAKE the minute we arrived in India by standing in the men-only line for frisking at airport security. A sari-clad woman clasped my elbow, yanked me behind the ladies' curtain, and gave me a thorough body scan by hand that the Memphis Police Department would be proud to claim. The first minutes of my first day evaporated as Rob and I deliberated how to get to the magical city of Darjeeling.

Railway lovers hold in their hearts the toy train up the mountains to that hill station. Narrow-gauged and very slow, the train carries passengers who peer like giants through the tiny windows as the engine slowly climbs through rhododendrons and cedars up to the tea plantations surrounding Darjeeling.

The bus—our choice—was faster and less expensive. Still it was twilight as we saw Darjeeling for the first time, lights twinkling like fairies up and down those curved steep streets as the bus groaned around the corner. The sparkle, and the altitude, took my breath away. So did the first English woman we met, Mrs. Marigold Wisdon.

I found her with the serendipity that lasted throughout our time in Asia. Looking for a place to change some dollars into rupees and a spot to spend the night, we were directed to the former Planters Club, now the Darjeeling Club.

A Sherpa servant walked us through the darkening hotel, along the second-story veranda to Mrs. Wisdon's apartment. Low ceiling, cozy, things of brass everywhere, all gleaming in the light of a coal fire, a space enlivened by half a dozen dogs. I almost sat on one. Mrs. Wisdon moved briskly into the room and offered us Room #1, but for one night only, because she was very busy.

I studied her face as she opened a "special temporary member" registration book.

Thin and in her 70s, she was formal and restrained, sparing only a few weak smiles. Her father's title had been First Commissioner of Darjeeling, whatever that meant. It must have been hard for her to rent rooms to "temporary members" after the glory days of the members-by-invitation-only Planters Club, at a time when the British retreated here for rest from battles and bureaucracy.

She dealt with her servants with excessive attention. She sent one of the shortest men I have ever seen down three switchbacks to "fetch the bags." With three pieces of luggage on his back, loaded like he was on an Everest expedition, the servant scampered back up the streets to the club. I accepted Mrs. Wisdon's hospitality, even at the high price of 200 rupees per night.

Then we entered the billiards room.

I don't remember many other people in there, but Deo Dixet was holding his billiard cue carefully. He saw Rob and me and came to chat.

Maybe life is lonely for a young tea-plantation manager in the hills of the Himalayas. But within a few minutes, he invited us to join him for the night. Would we like to come and see dawn from the tea fields beside the great peak Kanchenjunga? Yes!

We checked out of the Darjeeling Club faster than we had checked in.

Good night, Mrs. Wisdon.

From the hillside to a breakfast cup, the leaves of *Camellia sinensis*
cling to the mountainside near Kanchenjunga,
the border of India and Sikkim.

A Tea Plantation
in Darjeeling

I WOKE UP in the plantation guest room, snuggled beneath Tibetan blankets, to the sound of birds loud in the mimosa tree next to a flowering plum. Beyond, nothing.

Only air filled the three miles between me and the mountainside outside the window. I could now see the road we had driven from Darjeeling the night before, etched through miles of switchbacks and turns. The sun's angle showed the earth's crust sculpted with tea plants. The bushes did not cling to the side of the vertical slope. Instead they seemed to anchor the ground to keep it from levitating. Even rows, one pattern raking into another at an edge, a slope, a crest. Spheres of green camellia plants with fuzzy edges cordoned by trails for the pickers' feet. It looked from my height like a blanket of green corduroy.

About then I realized my swooning delight could be altitude giddiness.

Later that morning our host, Deo, walked us from the bungalow to the garden at the crest. Down below ran the Rangeet River, the border with the kingdom of Sikkim. Above it all, calm, impervious

Kanchenjunga—the giant peak, the world's third highest, soared above us.

One of three silent servants brought our first cups of Darjeeling tea to us on the veranda as we sat behind a row of marigolds, drinking in the scene.

I looked carefully at our host. Under a double-breasted navy blazer he wore a turtleneck and khakis. It seemed formal for a breakfast on the veranda.

Deo Dixit was a curious mixture of restraint and exuberance. At 28 years old, he was a year younger than me. Single, born in Kathmandu, educated in public schools in Darjeeling, he savored the English language and our American phrases. He wanted to hear every detail of our travels and what we thought of his corner of the world.

When he brought out his guitar and played as we talked, I realized we might be the rarity in his life, instead of the other way around.

What is it like to be him? I wondered. What does he have that leads him to pick up a traveling couple in the billiards room at the former Planters Club in Darjeeling? How often did that happen? Would his life expand to oversee multiple estates? His head for business was impressive. The Badamtam Tea Plantation produces 370 tons of tea per year, he told us, at 38 rupees per kilo, $3.80 for 2.2 pounds.

The tea itself tasted familiar and exotic at the same time. It was sharp, exciting. Like home, but closer, more intense, even a little bitter.

All the tins of Darjeeling tea I had ever seen in Alabama, Princeton, and Memphis, I could imagine again in looking at this cup of tea. The plants themselves flourished in sight of the highest mountains in the world, Everest to the west, and Kanchenjunga looming in the air in front of me.

After a long talk, I sensed Deo's mood return to the work of raising tea. Before he summoned a driver to take us back to Darjeeling, though he offered a tour of the barns and curing sheds.

Soon we were captivated by the details of manufacturing one of the best-known teas in the world: How pickers tug two leaves and a bud from the tips of the tea plant. How a pony lifts baskets of leaves to drying racks where they wither, curl, and ferment. Finally how workers carefully fire the tea in a slow oven, at 230 degrees, and pack the leaves in foil-lined balsa for shipping to tea connoisseurs around the world.

I felt giddy again, carried away. It's a good thing the breakfast tea was so strong, or on the spot I'd have thrown over my reporting career for a life as a tea queen.

A Shortcut Is Agony

*"The Himalayas rose layer upon layer until those
gleaming peaks proved a man to be so small that
it made sense to give it all up, empty it all out."*
—*Kiran Desai,* The Inheritance of Loss

B ADAMTAM UNDER the gaze of Kanchenjunga inspired us, confirmed our desire to trek closer up the mountain. But it took a dizzy day at 7,000 feet to get ready.

Mr. Das at the photo shop in Darjeeling sent us to find a day porter. He said we could find what we needed for three dollars a day at the Himal Ventures outfitting company. Which turned out to be two funny men running an office one story above the Polonia Hotel. If we'd hired one in advance from any American adventure tour company, the porter might have cost a hundred times more.

Our porter arrived. Dil Bahadour was a shy Nepali with eyes that crinkled up and down when he grinned. And he grinned constantly, even when he picked up our stuff. Telephoto lens, binoculars, Rob's shoes, books. We were well overprepared.

The Himal Ventures men rented us dollar-a-day

sleeping bags, and for 50 cents I borrowed an oversize North Face down jacket. It seemed a tiny price for so much warmth. But I did feel burrowed in, and my fingers poked out of the sleeves like anteaters.

The next morning we were off at 7:30, Dil leading us down and down to the bus station. A thong across the top of his head suspended a packed, top-heavy triangular basket. Rob and I wore tennis shoes, jeans, sweaters, and down.

Dil was bright in weird green trousers, an open jacket, and the kind of black leather shoes you'd see on the sidewalks of Manhattan. I could see no grip on the soles. But as we walked I noticed most of the Nepalis we met on the trail were barefoot.

Our route was supposed to be easy, a three-day jaunt for beginning trekkers looking for morning views of the mountain before late-day clouds obscured the sight. Before we could start though, we had to get to the trailhead. The bus was late; a tire had needed changing. We jolted 20 kilometers to Sukhia Pokhari, a squalid but genial town. For 30 cents we took a Land Rover to the border town of Maneybhanjang. Our goal for the first night of the trek was Meghma, a town 12 kilometers away and 4,000 feet above us.

We piled out. Dil took off up the only street in Maneybhanjang, and when the road curved to take the hill at an angle, he veered off and up.

"Shortcut," he said. That was his best English

phrase. I soon came to dread it. It was straight up, and it was agony.

In 10 minutes I'd lost my guilt over Dil carrying my luggage, and I was struggling. Sheep and goats had created that shortcut. Some tracks were too narrow for even the toe of my running shoes. I practiced sidestepping. It was no good. Tiny steps were great for my feet but rough for my breath. Toe walking felt better, if only for the relief it offered to my calves and Achilles tendon.

But Dil was not kidding about shortcuts. For an hour and a half we climbed the sheer mountainside, maybe 30 or 45 degrees up. No gentle curves, no angles, certainly no switchbacks.

Rob was red faced in 20 minutes, and when Dil stopped to rest, I bent over double to stretch my suffering hamstring muscles.

Dil watched me in sudden terror. He motioned to Rob. Was I throwing up?

Rob laughed, assuring him I was fine. I stretched out and stood up, but I don't think Dil ever trusted my stamina after that.

For the next three hours it never got easy, but it did become more peaceful. We took paths wide enough for a jeep with rhododendrons thick alongside the trail. Some held blue berries, an intense electric blue, pleasing against their green leaves.

The weather turned foggy and windy two thirds of

the way to Meghma. Suddenly, a stone house appeared on the mountain, the home of Nepali hill farmers. Dil motioned we should stop for tea. We stepped past chickens over a foot-high threshold and into the house, bending under the five-foot doorjamb, emerging into the red glare of the fire.

The ceiling was shiny black, ebonied from the tar in the wood smoke.

As my eyes adjusted to the dark, I saw copper pots, glasses, pans. We sat on splendid wool carpets laid on wooden platforms.

A woman, maybe 35, and her broad-faced young daughter brought us tea with milk. They set it down on tiny tables, not handing it to us directly. It was sweet, with leaves on the bottom.

Both women wore long, straight skirts circled with elaborate waists of heavy colorful woven strips. The older woman's waist was cinched with silver three inches wide, a hook on each end, centered with a bright blue turquoise stone.

She showed me the rugs she'd woven. They were small, narrow, and tightly knotted. Her daughter's rugs were brighter. Royal blue, orange, sky blue.

These wonders amazed me. In this dark room with its tiny windows and a shelf full of statues of Buddha, the colors glowed against the dirty floorboards,.

My curiosity intrigued them. The daughter beckoned me back to another room, also smoky and dark, where I spied a bundle of old sticks. At first I could only see their relationship to the rugs by the threads of wool caught in the splinters. Then I made out joints and shuttles. In that dust, under the tar-thick roof, I could imagine the young woman creating those warm patterns and happy colors.

There was nothing else in that house or those lives that I could see of beauty, or even diversion. The walls were papered with the *Statesman*, an Indian daily, yet no one here spoke English.

When we stopped for tea again on our way back down, the mother had a young son, maybe four years old, bring a bundle of smoking wood in a can into the room. She sat near the Buddhas twisting a string of beads with one hand. On the table in front of her she twirled a prayer wheel that pulled the smoke up into the ceiling. I looked closer and saw that the wheel was made from a soup can inside a quart oil can. Despite the rude containers, the care its maker used to create the prayer wheel was precise. It spun with a perfect balance.

But we had more mountain to climb up.

A Walker for Pleasure

W E SAW FEW other people on the final push up the mountain to Meghma. The fog was heavier and the boulders loomed up at me from the narrow path. This was no trade route. Only the folks who live here seemed to use the road, living on the odd tourist dollar and what they raised themselves. Not so different, I realized, from the Appalachian settlers still isolated in mountain pockets in Tennessee.

Only one other person was hiking like us. John was "a walker for pleasure," a Welshman who took a dim view of our prospects. John did not think we would reach the next trekking hut after Meghma in a single day.

Rob and I wrestled with the work of the climb and the cold and wondered if the weather would allow any views of Kanchenjunga to repay us.

The last steps to Meghma were a torture. But I could smell charcoal fires as we approached the trekking hut. Inside, four women in a dark kitchen brought tea, chapatis, four scrambled eggs, and fiery potatoes and onions. I threw the chapati on the coals, ash and all, as our fellow traveler John recommended. Surprisingly, it was not ashy-dusty but tasted smoky and strong.

Sitting there through a long twilight I watched the

women come and go. Men sat around another bed of coals. Their voices rose and fell. My legs stiffened and then gave way again. Thoughts came quiet, flowing. The hill was work, the air was thin. My body took over and reclaimed some peace.

Supper arrived at six, when the sun was long gone. The women served us on metal trays holding rice, more fiery potatoes, and a delicious salty bean soup that Dil poured onto his rice. With some ceremony a woman added two slices of purple onion to my plate, with a spoonful of coarse salt. The onion leaped through the roof of my mouth. It took three tablespoons of limp rice to put out the fire.

We drank water long boiled in that high altitude to make it safe. Best of all, the men offered Rob the local firewater, *tom bey*. It arrived in a wooden thermos with a wooden straw out the top. The center was filled with fermented millet, with boiling water poured on top. I insisted on a thermos for myself, and the women giggled.

It tasted nice, sweet, and a bit heady. Not beer at all and much gentler than scotch. Rob pronounced it "nothing." But it warmed me and did not give me a headache.

In 30 minutes we were asleep on the floor in North Face bags. Dead to the world and grateful.

Dawn, 6 a.m. Total mist world. All the spaces we had climbed to see were filled with opaque white. We ate bread and cheese and at eight o'clock made the sad decision to start climbing back downhill.

It was the right choice. I was not done with mountain trekking, but I was disappointed. To work this hard and be turned back by the weather? To go up would have been a miserable climb, with no views to sustain us. And, as Rob said, how many hours can you spend just looking at lichens?

So, down. The Nepali-Bengali frontier had its torments in that direction, too. Toes squashed against rocks, my left knee kicked back memories of falling off a bicycle onto the pavement of Tienanmen Square.

But it was easier to fall behind and enjoy the quiet. I heard two or three birds calling out of the fog. Trailing mosses on trees hung over vast plunges straight down. A cowbell rang out of nowhere.

We reached Darjeeling by midafternoon. We settled up with Dil, returned the sleeping bags, and spent the afternoon cozy in a room at the Budget Pine Ridge Hotel. It offered a hot shower, a nap, and time for writing. I was grateful.

Is Millet Beer
for Men Only?

THEY CALLED IT *tom bey* or *tomba*. After the night on the mountain I was determined to find out how to make it. Three young men taught me. They were showing tourists around the refreshment counter at the Tibetan Self-Help Refugee Centre in Darjeeling. I ordered a millet beer, and they talked as I sipped.

You start with millet, the same tiny grain we feed birds in America, they told me. Boil the millet just enough to crack open the seeds. Spread it out evenly to cool, and sprinkle over it what they called "medicine." All four of us struggled to translate that word. Finally we settled on the phrase "reaction maker." If I'd been a home brewer, I'd have known they were talking about a fermenting starter.

In Darjeeling they call the medicine *marchea*; packets are for sale in the town's marketplace.

Mix in the *marchea*, pack the millet carefully in anything. The young men pointed to plastic water jugs. A week later, after seven days in a warm place, it's ready to be packed in a thermos to have hot water poured over, and be sipped through a pierced bamboo pipe. Keep pouring on the water. Let it steep, drink it down, until nothing comes out but hot water. Then order another one.

I did not order another one. Instead, I moved on to the refugee center's women's carpet factory. It was delightfully cheery and warm. Children ran between the simple looms. I heard murmurs of talk among the women weavers. Most of the rugs wider than three feet were made by two women at once. They had to become pretty good friends to be able to sit side by side for the three weeks it usually took to create the rug.

Tibetan refugees spin thread for weaving carpets from piles of soft wool sheared from mountain sheep.

Taut white cotton warp slowly filled with bright-colored wool from wooden boxes holding colored skeins. The dance of the women's fingers was graceful and quick, slipping around the threads. Five women worked on a large 8x12-foot rug. One woman stood alone at the window, in the best light, wielding giant shears with metal handles covered in wool, sculpting the edges where one color met another. I leaned in to enjoy a close look at their work. Two women smiled back, fingers flying through the warp like harp players. One said, "You've had the *tomba*."

She laughed. I blushed.

"Naughty," she said. Then both of them giggled. "I can smell it. Nice."

Thanksgiving Greetings from Kathmandu

The Hotel Siddhartha, Kathmandu
Thursday, Thanksgiving

Dear Mom & Dad,

Imagine coming to Kathmandu to catch your breath! I thought this was one of the ends of the earth. But now I discover, compared to China and Darjeeling, I am in Western civilization again. No one stares at me on the street anymore. The shops here sell apple pie. Whatever happened to the remote Nepal of my imagination?

I may find out soon. Tomorrow, while you're recovering from turkey and cornbread dressing, Rob and I are taking the 6 a.m. express bus up out of Kathmandu toward the Annapurna range. We hope to have better success on our second trek than our first out of Darjeeling to see Kanchenjunga. Stories to tell! (Sob, I am homesick, really...)

Hong Kong was a strictly commercial buzz. But Thailand was artistic and lovely. We took an early visit to the floating markets in the Bangkok canals and stopped at a snake farm for the morning milking. I thought the cobra dance they performed was clearly for our benefit. Loved it anyway. The benefit does extend beyond the tourists on the Chao Phraya River. The venom I watched these Thai farmers milk from their poisonous cobras stocks the Memphis zoo with antivenin. I loved strolling Bangkok's jewelry district. Piles of rubies and sapphires gleamed from shop windows.

Rob bought me a ring, a smooth circle of jade. It is fun to travel with him. I love how he brings out the people we meet for easy conversation about their lives. He does cast a long shadow, though.

Our hotel in Bangkok was next to the Oriental Hotel, the famed expatriate home of writers Somerset Maugham, Noel Coward, and Joseph Conrad. The Oriental played up its former place in world letters with an Authors' Wing and an Authors' Bar with polished brass fixtures inviting you to tea. Enough to justify a $150-a-night room? We did not think so.

We took a third-class train into the country one day, to the old capital of Ayutthaya, now getting quietly eaten by a Thai version of kudzu.

Lots of water buffalo cruised in the rice fields beside the train, looking like a peaceful scene from the Vietnam War. But the fellow next to Rob let us know the peacefulness was deceptive. We had been warned not to take third-class trains, but we hadn't worried because this was just a short trip. Then this guy who looked like he could whip any tough from rough parts of Montevallo or Memphis pulled his necklace from his shirt. He asked us if we had one, too. Dangling in a glass tube was a two-inch piece of carved wood covered in gold leaf. He let us know it was his amulet, protection against the bandits who stop the train and chop off peoples' heads. Terrific. Our stop was next, and we scrambled.

We missed Burma, my fault, on the way from Thailand to India. I messed up by a day the date for the once-a-week flight. We even had visas stamped in our passports. I knew I'll regret it one day. Rob is not letting me forget it now! But Burma has a really bad image on the road here: It's the only socialist country west of Vietnam. The economy is in shreds, and dangerous black marketeers are everywhere, we keep hearing. I would've loved a boat ride up the Irrawaddy River to Mandalay or at least loved telling about it. Dad, the Frank Sinatra version of Kipling's poem is still singing in my head, reminding me of you.

Come you back to Mandalay
Where the old flotilla lay
Can't you hear their paddles chonkin'
From Rangoon to Mandalay?
On the road to Mandalay
Where the flyin' fishes play
And the dawn comes up like thunder
Out of China 'cross the bay

When we left Calcutta for Nepal, the airline pilots had a secret treat in store. Twenty minutes away from Kathmandu, flying in some hazy clouds, the stewardess whispered a question. Would we like to join the pilots in the cockpit. Would we! In about two seconds we were in the cockpit. The haze was clearer. And we were staring straight at Mount Everest. I could not believe my eyes.

Sitting in a bed of clouds, its peak a bit higher than closer mountaintops. Off to the east, much more distinctive, was Kanchenjunga. The cockpit view was awesome and terrifying. I could see Annapurna, K2, Everest, all the world's highest mountains, like a mouth full of teeth just waiting for Indian Air Flight 177.

We took a sharp right. A saucer opened up beneath the plane. Miles across, and a long way down, sat Kathmandu. It looked small, almost pitiful from the air. We were at 10,000 feet, Everest in front of us at 29,000.

Just as we flew over the lip of that saucer, I heard the warning system of the plane switch on. A recorded voice in urgent Federal Aviation Authority English warned the pilot, "Pull up, pull up." The pilot ignored it. We coasted down. He lined the plane up with another massive peak he said they have not bothered to name yet and welcomed us to Kathmandu.

We staggered out after the pilot encouraged us to swap some English dollars for rupees. Then I realized his generous invitation to the cockpit was an opportunity for him to benefit from some informal currency exchanges without the usual fee.

Everest disappeared from sight. But I didn't care.

The sun was dropping. We were in the valley, and I knew the mountains lay behind it.

I miss you folks a lot. Why is it the international FAA voices recorded in airplanes always sound like they're from Shelby County? That southern twang made me realize how far from home we are.

LOVE,
SALLY

Sharp edges and shadows from the world's highest mountains
stretch to the far horizon

The first donkey in a train of pack animals wears a high plume
and musical bells to lead others down a rocky trail.
Nepali women walking up the trail give them plenty of room.

TOWARD ANNAPURNA

KATHMANDU was a fun dirty mix of monkeys and reminders of 1960s free love and drugs. After a day or so, we were ready to try another trek for a view of the great peaks.

On the far end of a bus ride from Kathmandu, we found a guide to hike with us toward Annapaurna. Kazi came with good English, an impish smile, and deep knowledge of the trails through the mountain passes.

We planned a circular route whose names twisted in my mouth with adventurous sounds: Pokhara, Birethanti, Naudanda, Mustang, and the fishtail-shaped peak of Machapuchare. The mountain is revered by Nepalis. The government does not permit hikers to reach its summit.

So the three of us set out to climb around it. On the trail we walked with three Tibetan women, heavily loaded, with a baby. They'd left Mustang, on the border with China, and were headed for Pokhara. They walked slowly, balancing filled baskets on their backs with careful steps. All wore long dark skirts and blouses with colorful aprons in front. We walked faster than they did, but they passed us during a rest stop.

I wanted a photograph. We had seen a few small groups of women on the trail, eyes clear but cast down. I'd noticed brass nose rings, ears outlined with gold and jewels. But especially I'd seen their coral and turquoise necklaces.

I asked for a photo with a gesture and my camera. The oldest woman brushed me aside, and they kept climbing. We overtook them at a corner. We smiled. Many caravans of ponies came down past us along with several other trekkers. Three hundred feet higher we met them again. It was a lunch stop for the baby. By now I did not want to photograph them. I had admired their climb. Their faces. Kazi chatted, as much as he was capable of chatting given his taciturnity, and I admired the baby.

Mother was short, not 4 feet 10. Grandmother watched. I went to her. Her wrinkled face and high broad cheeks reminded me of Edward Curtis photos of American Comanches. When she let me, I held her necklace. I twisted each fine piece of coral. They were big as cherries, the color of tangerines. Four flat blue pieces of turquoise lay between the coral. In her ears, another turquoise stone was the size of my thumbnail. A knotted thread through her ear tied the stone to another jewel, a piece of orange coral.

Then she took my hand. She moved the jade ring Rob gave me in Bangkok. She murmured something. She twisted it three times around, patted my arm, then stroked my arm, smiling. I was wearing a filthy T-shirt. I'd worn it for three days and felt its coat of grime. But she wanted to say something. She would not let my arm go. So Kazi translated for us. "Clean," she says. "You feel so clean and nice. For her, so hard to be clean. So hard."

The famous fishtail at the top of the peak named Machapuchare seems to follow a creature swimming straight down into the roots of the earth.

Later, from a Tibetan health worker for Save the Children, I learned how harmful dirt can be. She said cooking smoke and dirt particles coat the lungs of people living here; it's among the greatest threats to children's health in the Himalayas.

The grandmother was as dirty as everyone else we had seen on the trail, as dusty as we were. She had lines of dust in the folds of her neck, smoke in her clothes, grit in her ears, just like me. But my dirt was fresh. Hers had accumulated over a lifetime. I never imagined how just being dirty predicted a lifetime of health problems. What was ahead for the baby? I patted the old woman's shoulder. We walked on ahead.

Four or five times more that day we passed each other at resting corners. Each time the older woman smiled. When we stopped at Naudanda, they passed us the last time, heading down the hill toward Pokhara.

Two Nepali girls demonstrate how a bandanna
can resemble their flowing head scarves if the
wearer can just learn how to tie it.

FERTILIZER IS LIKE HEROIN

T HE MOUNTAINS AROUND Kathmandu are little hills compared to the giant peaks of the Himalayas. I was getting familiar with saying, "him-MAHL-yahs," trying to sound like the expatriates who had been there a while. But if I wanted to see one of those giant peaks as the sun rose, I had to get out of the Kathmandu valley and up onto the saucer of hills around it.

Rob and I took a bus one afternoon through the countryside, slowly climbing past terraced farms and roadside temples, passing barefoot women in long tribal skirts threshing millet, toward the town of Dhulikhel to get up early for the view.

Our bus mates included Tony and Paddy Long.

Tony was a half-Polish, half-Sussex farmer, big, good looking. His wife, Paddy, was a pale American, shrunk into a padded jacket and suffering from dysentery. I did not smile when she told me what ailed her, but I couldn't help thinking that nobody on this side of the world ever seems to admit to anything simple, like diarrhea. It is either dysentery, hepatitis, or something else even worse. She said it was a mosquito bite in Delhi that gave her dengue fever and malaria, and it well could have been.

Because of her, I vowed to be a little more serious about those funny big candy pink malaria pills prescribed for me back home.

We fell into the quick confidences expatriates and travelers can exchange in a few scant hours on a shared bus ride. Paddy told me she taught English in primary and middle schools around the world but not with the Peace Corps or any other group that she says "enforces begging." She used to teach at a 1960s citadel for cultural revolution, the Milky Way School in Amsterdam. Then she gave up on the Dutch.

Scornful and cheerful all at once, her opinions were stronger than she seemed to be. I began to sense Paddy wouldn't wear well. Perhaps that explained why she and Tony were always on the move.

They seemed to have lived everywhere. Tony dispensed travel advice with quick, memorable sentences. Yes, he said, we should go to Ladakh. "Naked geography, absolutely gorgeous, nature with her clothes off." I promised myself to see if he was right.

It made sense he claimed to be a freelance writer, his subject nature. When I pressed him for a topic, he said, "Oh, the woodlands of Europe." After that vague wave off, he admitted that in between writing assignments, he moves money for friends. That's when I began to notice the drug imagery in his stories.

"Farm fertilizer here. It's addictive. Like smack."

That is how Tony began his version of the arrival of fertilizer in the Kathmandu hills.

First, an agriculture advisor arrives in the dry season, like right now. As he told this story, Tony gestured out the bus window to the Nepali fields in December. The newly arrived advisor sees brown hills and orders fertilizer. Free bags of ammonium nitrate and urea arrive from the US. The Brahmins receiving the fertilizer charge the Nepali farmers a dollar a sack.

They buy and are amazed at the results. So they abandon their ancient compost-fertilizer system and get hooked on these new chemicals coming in bags from the United States.

Then Brahmins raise the price to $10 a bag. The old compost heaps are gone. The Nepali peasants have to spend ten times their rupees on what was supposed to be free farm aid. And that is when Tony says the Peace Corps volunteer shows up. In dismay the Peace Corps worker says, "Lord, they don't even know how to fertilize with compost," and begins a dung program.

But by then, the old ways are forgotten, the worn-out soil needs the amendments, the Brahmins won't quit making money off the supposedly free chemicals, and, of course, the king is tied in. Soon everybody is somehow begging.

Tony and Paddy said they had fallen out of love with Nepal. She said it was becoming a nation of beggars. Sure enough, she whispered as we parted, they planned to leave Nepal soon to move to India. To Dharamsala, the town where the Dalai Lama fled into exile.

Just before the sun came up, we walked from a trekking hotel up a wide dusty path to the edge of the saucer. Even in the dark I could sense the outline of the peaks. The big dipper was bright above us. A crescent moon suggested a new month. We'd been promised a 180-degree view of the mountains, 100 miles of snowy peaks. A dozen kinds of birdcalls greeted the sun as it arrived in pink glory against a violet sky. Slowly an icy outline appeared, long, thin, and jagged. Everest on the right, Langtang, a dozen others, Annapurna way out on the left, too far away to be more than an edge. A faint wind picked up dust and warmed my nose.

I picked out the glaciers with binoculars. Rob and I exhausted our cameras lenses. Then we climbed down to breakfast and the bus ride back to Kathmandu.

One afternoon we set out for St. Xavier's School, in a prime minister's palace a few miles from Kathmandu. I wanted to find a Jesuit priest named Father Moran. He was a ham radio buddy of my engineer friend George Alsobrooks at the TV station in Memphis. George knew Father Moran by his famous ham call sign, 9N1MM. He called it Nine En One Mickey Mouse, and sure enough, the priest was world famous among ham aficionados as the only one transmitting from Nepal when the kingdom was closed to most outsiders. During earthquakes and mountain disasters, Father Moran's voice was often the only source of news for the rest of the world to hear.

I knew he'd founded the school and hoped to hear from him a more tolerant attitude toward Nepalis.

Sadly, Father Moran himself was on sabbatical in Simla. Instead, his priests gave us brown bread and a tour of the buffalo-dung methane water heaters. They told us Father Moran was the first Christian allowed into the Kingdom of Nepal to teach in 1950, under orders that he not convert people. He flew in the first books in 1951, creating a school that to this day is the finest in Nepal, a training ground for the sons of royalty and first families. But still no Christian converts.

I wondered if the learned Jesuits struggled with that, but they didn't say.

Tony and Paddy's stories stayed with me. I was curious to know if other expatriates saw things differently. The chance to ask came up a few nights later.

When we arrived in Kathmandu, I had looked up a friend's connection with the Voice of America folks. A generous invitation to dinner followed, and Bob, a big-deal ornithologist, came to pick us up.

Bob steered his right-hand-drive VW, special ordered from Germany, to Patan, to the westernmost home in the most wealthy suburb in the Kathmandu valley. It hid behind high fences, with military officers and ministers as neighbors.

The house was full of stuffed birds and plants collections and Western furniture. That means they had chairs. Each chair had warm blankets in easy reach.

But no heat. No heat. No heat!

Why? No firewood in the valley, impure kerosene chokes its users, and electricity is new and unreliable.I was glad to drape a blanket over my lap.

A host of servants passed a feast of roast pork, fresh cauliflower, mashed potatoes and gravy, and fresh coconut cream pie. The talk was even better than the dinner.

Bob and his wife, Linda, sadly admitted to having few close Nepali friends. They said the Nepalis demand too much. Like help getting children into special schools like St. Xavier's, like help getting visas.

They said corruption here was growing daily and they would not be surprised at Indian absorption of Nepal.

Pay attention at the post office, they recommended. Watch the line of Nepalis making sure the stamps are canceled by hand. Otherwise they fear clerks will peel them off to sell them again, and the letters will go undelivered.

Another couple at dinner that night had served with the United States Information Service for three years in Nepal, raising three redheaded sons there.

This officer with the world's biggest PR agency promoting the world's most powerful nation was amazingly candid. It's not just the top levels of Nepali society pushing for favors, Jack said. The bottom is corrupt, too. But the king sets the example, and he's rotten to the core.

Curiosity shines from the eyes of the young girl wrapped to carry her brother on the way to Annapurna.

All the rural aid coming to this rural country? Only half gets to the farmers; fully 35 percent of it stays in Kathmandu, he added. I was amazed by the precision of his numbers and asked if American oversight could correct this.

He laughed. Not in our own local interests, he said. US enforcement overseers overlook the mishandling because their own jobs are built into it. Why risk canceling your own program? It offers a high-paying job in an inexpensive country with a staff of five to ten, not counting the guards. How can you clean up others when your own house is untidy?

Our hosts went quiet as we talked about begging and aid. They only want to lead people through the birds and natural beauty of this part of the earth, they said. And on a year-to-year visa, they must stay in favor with the king. Their own subtle beg was to be quiet.

A wealthy farmer uses four beasts to thresh grain on a tiny cultivated ledge near Pokhara, Nepal.

CHRISTMAS IN A BUDDHIST KINGDOM

DEAR FAMILY,

I will never have another Christmas like this. It has been wonderful, exotic and very far from home. I got a little sad at being so distant from the people who are my Christmas. Then I resolved to wait and share Christmas with you after all in March, when I get home.

So here's how it went. Christmas Eve we left our houseboat on Lake Dal, the jewel in the Vale of Kashmir, and set out for the military airport. Our goal was the last valley in India, part of the Tibetan plateau, 11,500 feet high.

Trouble is, the road between the valleys is only open four months a year, and the plane ride over four major Himalayan ranges only flies twice a week.

We had tried on Wednesday. Rain in Kashmir, snow in Ladakh. Indian Air canceled.

But that meant they gave us a free night and meals at the best hotel in town! The $35 room for a canceled $20 flight was a real deal. Plus reliable hot water.

On Friday the air was clear. The crowd at the airport excited me. There were two large Tibetan-looking men in woolen coats to their ankles with mandarin collars and red sashes. Five or six men wore Astrakhan hats, reminding me how close to the Soviet Union we were. I'd last seen hats like that in Moscow, in Omsk, in Irkutsk.

I wondered how I could be so excited to get to a place I'd never heard of three months before. Would it reveal, as Tony Long had claimed in Nepal, "Naked geography, absolutely gorgeous, nature with her clothes off"?

The plane was packed with Indian military coming to the border patrol. Pakistan and China are both about 10 miles away. The troops looked miserable. The pilot delayed half an hour, waiting for weather reports from the valleys. When we took off, my camera wedged against a window, we saw nothing for half an hour. Then, snow on mountains and spectacular views. Finally, we curved steeply between two ridges and slid to a stop next to an Indian Air Force plane, Russian made, a gun turret in its tail.

The airstrip was slanted. Troops ran from a rude building to push chocks under the wheels so we would not roll backward into the headwaters of the Indus River.

The mountains were bare-bones, dusty, like the moon. Moisture cannot clear the high peaks, so most of the snow stays west. Tony Long was right.

In this fierce valley 5,000 monks live in stone-cold monasteries nestled on the sides of the cliffs. Today we visited three. *Gompas*, they call them. Saw the monks at prayer, beside strange golden statues of Buddha, young eight-year-old monks in red robes with shaved heads, all curious and eager to see us.

There are Christians in this valley. But not many. After 300 years of trying, I'm told, Moravian missionaries managed to convert maybe 20 families. So our guide took us to see the town's lone Christmas tree. It was precious.

Ice grows on the headwaters of one of the world's great rivers. The Indus begins its journey in an icy stretch of water in the Himalayas before flowing through the hot heart of India.

For Christmas Eve dinner, noodles and Tibetan mutton dumplings. But on the way home from the dining stall to our guesthouse, the only one left open for the winter, the stars were brilliant. The moon was half full, shining on a thin scrape of snow. Way up the mountain, I saw three little lights in an icy monastery. I could hear distant chanting. Rob and I sang Christmas carols to the moon. "O holy night! The stars are brightly Shining" never felt so true. "Silent Night" moved me to tears. I'm weeping now as I remember it again.

We shared oranges and walnuts with two friends we had met in Kashmir and who had flown with us to Ladakh. Just like Christmas stockings at home, simple gifts. Gunther the German had oranges and walnuts, apples and coconut macaroons. We contributed almonds, cashews, and apricots. I've never had a holiday like this one!

Rob is super to travel with. He is enthusiastic about the same dumb things I am. Plus his height and presence have sailed us past a million problems. Now if the airport here will just stay open enough for us to get out!

MUCH LOVE,
SALLY

Prayer flags mark a busy commercial street in Leh, Ladakh,
beneath the walls of the Chandazik Gompa and royal palace.

A WEALTHY MAN ON THE
ROOF OF THE WORLD

CHRISTMAS DAY IN Ladakh was clear and lonesome, high in the Himalayas on the edge of China, a tiny sliver of India pressed between uncertain borders with Tibet and Pakistan.

We found a good guide in Tashi, who found us a family to stay with and guided us around the valley. He had a taste for self-promotion, a friendly procurer who claimed to have led a group of Canadians around Everest, who knew the traditional herbalist doctor, who knew which curtained door on the main street of Leh would lead to a supper of mutton dumplings. On Christmas afternoon he led us to the home of the wealthiest man in Ladakh to pay respects.

Mutub Coloan greeted us with Kashmiri tea. A cardamom pod floated in the cup. Not for this worldly man the Tibetan tea with yak butter I'd drunk in the stalls on the main street. He beckoned us to his back room, a high-ceilinged space with single-pane windows filled with views of the peaks of the Ladakhi range. The room was bare, unfurnished except for a magnificent carpet.

He slowly seated himself on it. He was thin, maybe 60 years old, I thought, from the deep grooves the sun and the altitude had worn into his face. My guess of his age, I discovered later, was shy by a good 15 years.

When he began to talk, I forgot I was irritable from the cold and dizzy from the altitude at 12,000 feet. I sat on my knees on that rug like a supplicant and listened to what this man's life had been.

He told me he'd started as a boy helping his father with a string of pack animals and trading beyond the mountain range to the east. They would take apricots to the Tibetans and trade for wool. He pointed out the window to some scrawny trees huddled against the bank of the Indus. Apricot trees, he said, which soften the sky in the spring and draw sweetness from the sharp sun of the short Ladakhi summer.

In the fall women gathered the fruit and dried it on the flat roofs of the houses, spreading it out in a rosy carpet next to the shrines of Buddha on each family's roof. They turned the apricots in the sun, turning the prayer wheels at the same time, making the task at once practical and faithful.

Mutub and his father loaded the animals—yaks, donkeys, some ponies—and carried the dried apricots to the top of the mountain range. But never down the other side. There was no other side to these mountains. It was the great Tibetan plateau. Mutub's customers camped in seasonal settlements across the broad high plain that stretches thousands of miles to Mongolia.

Mutub traded the apricots for fine pashmina wool.

One kilogram of apricots bought four kilograms of pashmina. It was a handsome trade for all involved. Tibetans valued apricots for the variety they added to a thin diet of barley and potatoes. Plus, the apricot pits held a rich oil, used as a balm and a source of calories. The Tibetans paid in pashmina, a wool from the soft chest hairs of wild mountain goats. It was gathered by hand, sometimes tugged from scrub bushes on the cliffs where the goats grazed.

I had held a pashmina shawl in a bazaar in Kashmir. It cost 8,000 rupees, $800 for a floating fabric maybe five feet square. In a burst of salesmanship the owner had tugged a silver ring from his little finger and pulled the scarf through with a magician's flourish. It was astonishingly warm for its weight. I could see why pashmina was valued so highly in these cold mountains.

With Mutub's animals staggering under the weight of the wool, he hurried back down the passes through Ladakh and on to the bazaars of Kashmir. Here a kilo of pashmina was worth 40 kilograms of apricots. Year after year he made the trip, inheriting his father's animals, adding more, sometimes trading farther to the west. I was beginning to understand his profits. One to 4, then 4 to 160. A fabulous return for a trip over the world's highest mountains.

Two months from Ladakh to Tibet, one month for trading, two months back, a month to rest, six weeks to Kashmir or Baltistan or the Karakoram, six weeks back, time out for bad weather. Then the year began again in April when the passes cleared. Once he traveled as far as Turkestan, where he traded his entire cargo of wool for this one carpet we were sitting on.

I looked again beyond my knees. A riot of maroon and blue, 18 feet long by 8 feet wide, finely knotted into elaborate borders and flowers. Was that a hint of China in the crenellated border? A bit of Persia in the stylized flowers?

It was the middle of the 1940s, he'd forgotten which spring, when the British came. They had special favors to ask. Bundles to be carried across the mountains. Small bundles, lumps really, wrapped in brown jute. He recognized that the jute came from Burma. But he did not know what it held. The British told him not to open any bundles, told him the deal he was to strike when he got where they asked him to go.

He loaded his 50 animals with the brown packages. He never let his men unload them, even once, on the weeks of travel over the mountains and beyond. Mutub went farther than he had ever gone across the Tibetan plateau. On and on across the highlands, clear to Hotan on the lip of the Xinjiang desert.

He was met by Chinese men wearing the uniform of the Nationalist army. They unloaded his packs and weighed out the parcels on great brass scales. Kilo for kilo with Mongolian gold.

What were the British sending to Chiang Kai-shek's officers in the farthest corner of China? So precious and so secret it was worth its weight literally in gold?

He found out then that he had delivered opium, grown by the British in Burma, to feed Chiang Kai-shek's increasing certainty that only opium would keep the people away from the appeal of Mao.

The opium on his pack train would've lasted a decade in that thinly populated part of China, Mutub said. But of course it was not enough. The corruption of the Nationalist troops made sure the opium was too costly for all but the wealthy. And the wealthy were not likely to be swayed by Mao's popular appeal.

I asked Mutub if he ever actually saw anyone using the opium. Yes, he nodded vigorously. The official in charge of unloading it, right there on the spot filled a pipe and then... Mutub made a floating gesture with his hands.

He came home to Ladakh a seriously wealthy man. He did not tell me what happened to the gold or how much the British waiting for him paid.

He said after that he made a few more runs across the mountains. But the pashmina-apricot trade seemed a bit tame to him by then.

And a few years later, in 1950, the Chinese invaded Tibet. They sealed the border in 1959 as the Dalai Lama escaped into exile. No more pashmina flowed through Ladakh. That was the end of his trips east over the mountains. And then the Indian and Pakistani border wars cut off his trips beyond Srinagar and Kashmir. He sold off his pack animals, one by one, and settled into a quiet life. He watched his children and grandchildren grow up and go down into India to be educated.

One son, he said, is idly considering building a ski slope along the passes between Ladakh and Srinagar. Wouldn't that be a nice diversion? I don't think he really expected an answer.

I wondered if Mutub ever had any regrets about carrying the opium for the British. I wondered if he regretted serving that particular master. If in some Buddhist center of himself, he thought that act of evil against the Chinese people had somehow brought on the overwhelming retribution of the invasion of Tibet. But I wondered about that later. At that moment, I sat and watched the sun slide behind the mountains and the scratchy shadows of the apricot trees disappear from the headwaters of the Indus River.

ELLORA AND AJANTA

WE STAYED IN Aurangabad for two days to see the religious cave carvings in Ellora and Ajanta. Our first day, at Ellora, was wonderful. We crossed the tail of a mountain range, and curved alongside it in a choking tourist bus. When we arrived, the driver gestured. "The caves are there. You can have them." He seemed eager to join fellow drivers at the tea stall and be rid of all of us. The other tourists on the bus moved in a line toward the dark spaces full of holy art; Hindu, Jain, and Buddhist symbols sitting beside each other in a happy mingling of faiths.

The Buddhas were big and dark. The statues loomed even larger as my eyes opened to take them in. A delicious low-impact answer to lighting the carvings came from a dozen men holding mirrors. These mirror–wallahs stood at the lip of the cave and reflected the sun onto the idols' faces. Then they hit you for a rupee as you stumbled out. The whole afternoon was a contest between stumbling feet and dilating eyes. The friendly commingling of commerce and faith continued at the soft drink patio where a goat wandered in to nose our Thums Up drinks.

The Ajanta cave trip began the next day, with another driver and a fresh crowd of tourists. It started well, but at a stop for tea, Rob began to feel sick. By the time we got to Ajanta, he was in the grip of it. After cave number one he gave up and went back to the bus to wait in the hot sun and be near the toilet. The caves at Ajanta were older, with none of the mingled faiths of Ellora. All were dedicated to Buddha. Created over hundreds of years, these statues were carved and abandoned before A.D. 500 and not rediscovered by the world until 1819.

I expected reverence. Instead, the caves were hot and full of noisy children, shouting guides, and over-eager mirror-wallahs. I overheard them give Hindu names and attributes like Death-Destroyer God and Preserver God to the Buddha and his Bodhisattvas. They even let Lord Vishnu help in Buddha's birth! It was as wrong as letting Matthew, Mark, Luke, and John help Moses get the Israelites out of Egypt.

I couldn't straighten all this out and got angry and ran ahead of the group. I found more kids and more yelling, until in the last cave I encountered the best of what had become a miserable day. Dying Buddha, lying on his side, 20 feet long, one cheek sagging. The carver in 200 B.C. even compressed the stone pillow underneath his head. It moved me, the humanity of that flattened stone pillow by the holy head of Buddha. I stayed for a long time.

When I got back to the bus, Rob was in bad shape. The Chatterjees, a nice couple from Poona, were responsible for two of the squealers in the caves. They offered medicine and helped me swap our cramped backseat on the bus for the very front, so Rob could stretch out. I had to crawl up front and sit in the aisle beside the driver.

We drove fast, over a rough road back to Aurangabad. There was nothing for me to lean on. I swayed and stared through the windshield. In the sinking sun I saw two buses stopped on the roadside. Just as we passed, my fingers in my ears against the inevitable awful air horn, an old man stepped out between the buses, and we hit him.

The driver wrenched to the right, braking. Stopped. I was by the door and out, running back 50 yards. The man was not dead. He was sitting up, blood pooling around his leg and head. We laid him back down. Our bus driver carried him, turban wrapped, to the bus.

We drove fast to the nearest doctor. It was horrible. The cut on the man's head sliced clear across his eyebrows. He'd seen the bus at the last minute and jumped back but not fast enough. The jump probably saved his life, but I didn't know that yet.

Mr. Chatterjee said the old man would have been left for dead by most drivers, certainly every private Tata trucker. Too long to wait for police, too troublesome the official machinery of faultfinding. But our driver looked worried for the old man. As a government tourist bus driver, he had a duty to help. It felt like an hour before we found the doctor in the town where we had stopped for tea that morning. Both doctor and hospital were basic. The doctor was 35 to 40 years old, potbellied, with a harassed face but focused eyes. He and a nurse in a white sari washed their hands in green American antiseptic juice and cleaned and stitched the old man's head. I kept replaying the moment, feeling the thud of the bus against his body. I asked the doctor how he would be, and he answered simply, "Fine."

So we sat in the bus, relieved, waiting for the police to come and finish with the driver. I played with the two Chatterjee children. They told me moronic jokes I had not heard for years. Here's one. The daughter holds up her finger. Why doesn't Ravi Shankar play with this finger? Why? Because it's my finger! Ha ha ha! The whole bus laughed.

The police finished, and three orderlies brought the old man back to the bus. An old woman, a relative, had materialized and sat on the step at his feet. We were to take him to the big hospital in Aurangabad, where they say the wards are not filthy rooms of string beds with families living around the patients. The man's turban was white gauze this time. An orderly rode with him. Rob and I sat up with the driver again. I looked back once. They were taking his pulse, and the relative was crying into a corner of her sari.

Peasants, Mr. Chatterjee told me, shaking his head.

They've never seen trucks. They have no idea how fast a bus can go. Then Mr. Chatterjee frowned. This is a calamity for that man. What if he loses his shoes? Will he have the money to return to his village?

That made the whole accident even worse. I offered to collect donations from the other tourists on the bus. Can we gather some money to help him get back home? I asked. The Chatterjees put a few bills in my hand. No one else did. I walked up and down the aisle, but nobody would look me in the eye. When we reached Aurangabad, the orderly carried him off the bus.

I felt really American. I gave the old woman 60 of our rupees. Six dollars. She cried again.

Mail call in the mountains—Kathmandu's American Express office
let travelers collect messages and updates from family and friends at home.

An Elephant Hunts
a Rare Rhino

Dear Perdita,

As I rode my elephant yesterday, I thought of you. How often can I start a letter like that? You'd have laughed at the sight of your granddaughter weaving above the tall grass, swaying from an elephant invisible beneath her in the tall grasses.

We hunted on elephant back by the Rapti River, on the central border of India and Nepal. Our target? The great one-horned rhinoceros facing extinction. There were 10 of us in all, riding five elephants, which slowly lumbered through the grass.

A movement to the left. A deer jumped! It leaped higher than the head of my elephant. He stopped dead still, and when something as big as an elephant doesn't move, that is dead still. The afternoon sun shone with brutal force. I saw clouds of bright green parrots with red bills shift uneasily from one tree to another and back.

The driver nudged the elephant out of his stance. I held the elephant's shoulder and felt his enormous bulk shift from leg to leg. His skin was heavy and dry with unpleasant hairs poking out like old whiskers on a porcupine. At every step his skin slid—too much skin for the body inside. We moved in a big circle, creating arcs in the grass. In the quiet the noise of flapping elephants' ears crackled like newspapers, spanking against my ankle.

And then I saw movement under the grass. A snout appeared with pink eyes. The elephant saw it, too, and stopped. Rob tightened his grip behind me. The snout lifted and showed teeth. We were 15 feet from the ugliest ancient rhino a cartoonist could draw. His mouth gaped open, dribbling stems of grass.

His horn stuck up like a pug dog's. Or like cousin Connie, when she tapes her nose tip to her forehead to make a pig face. The rhino's eyes were so close to the horn he looked cross-eyed.

But his head was almost insignificant compared to his body. A Sherman tank! The elephant moved closer. The rhino shifted away. Other elephants circled, and we flushed him out of the grass up 30 feet to a rise. The rhino pawed and shook its head in pink-eyed fury. I suddenly remembered how rhino hunts staged by maharajas often end with the rhino chasing the elephant.

I hung on tight. We moved closer. The elephant didn't seem to like that idea and started making growling elephant noises. By now we had the rhino in a hundred-foot circle of elephants.

One hundred years ago, maybe only 50, or even 10, that rhino would be a rug right now. His horn sold for its weight in gold to the Asian drug market. Rhino-horn powder is thought to be the ultimate aphrodisiac, but so is rhino urine. (I couldn't imagine anybody standing around with a cup to catch this rhino's urine.) Then he wheeled around fast, faster than you can think a creature with the bulk of a garage wheeling. He ran through the circle up to the trees and escaped. We all hooted. Shouting, pounding our drivers on their backs, rubbing the elephants' gross shoulders. It was splendid. Up close to a dangerous disappearing species and safe to tell the tale.

For another hour we rode through the woods and grasses, happy and quiet, watching the sun sink behind India. We flushed three kinds of deer, saw the prints of a Bengal tiger, watched for the dens of sloth bears. Three peacocks flew in front of us as we slouched toward home.

That night, around a bonfire at the Chitwan Royal Game Preserve, Tharu tribesman danced a Hindu war dance for us. That's what they called it, and I believed it. Sixteen men performed for us and four other visitors. They waved sticks and shouted as they danced. That nine of them were barefoot did not surprise me. But seven wore high-top black basketball sneakers, Chuck Taylors, just like brother-in-law David Rosenberg. Somehow the Chuck Taylors did not destroy the illusion of a Hindu war dance. They were fierce.

Kerosene and candles only out here, no hot water.

And, yes, Perdita, Rob is a good traveling companion. He sends his best. He writes in his journal and reads as much as I do, so we never bore or bother each other. This trip may take a little longer than I expected. But having no schedule does clear me from the thought of deadlines. I miss you and wish you'd been on that elephant with me. How we would have laughed together!

BIG HUGS,
SALLY

III
THE PACIFIC

*"While we are editing our trails,
our trails are also editing us."*
—ROBERT MOOR

Okay, Perth!

ICAN GET REALLY enthusiastic about this town. It seemed easy to live in. Safe, clean, calm traffic, lots of pedestrians casually dressed and walking with a purpose. For the first time in half a year I could read all the billboards. So I did, and of course, my eyes were soon aching from the relentless barrage of Promotional English.

I soaked up the contrast with Asia. No bright saris, no more men in long skirts.

Suddenly, all the men were in khaki shorts and kneesocks. Never seen so many revealing tank tops on women. It made me uncomfortable, after the decorum of India and Sri Lanka. Too healthy, almost.

Rob and I wandered the streets happily all that first day. We spotted a restaurant named the Magic Apple, the first natural food restaurant either of us had seen in the 11,000 miles since the Squash Blossom in Memphis. Behind us in line were two guys named John and Rob. I heard the flat clean tones of John's Nebraska accent, and we four were friends by the end of lunch.

We arranged to picnic the next day on the Swan River. John picked us up at noon with his daughter, Elizabeth, and her friend in tow. Rob's daughter, Gemma, came with him. A splendid pier on the Swan gave us a good view of the cruise boats out on the Perth Water, tidal backup of the Swan River mouth.

The Perth Water had jellyfish, which discouraged us from swimming. So the girls got me to rent them a paddleboat. I loved it, enjoying the unfamiliar motherly sense of paddling with young girls, laughing and packing up the remains of salad fixings and juice and cake. The afternoon stayed cool, blue, clear.

I watched the men warm to Rob, be taken and dazzled by his personality and stories. I was happy, proud to have met them and to have brought us together after that long spell in India when I seemed to meet no one. The afternoon seemed to have charmed everyone. John offered a tour, eager to stay with us, to listen, but also to talk. His story, like that of Tony and Paddy Long in Kathmandu, was full of short stays and restlessness.

He came from Nebraska to Harvard, studied linguistics in California, served with the Peace Corps in Africa, and now seemed confused about his future. He'd taught psychology at Western Australia University as a visiting professor but felt squeezed out when the program ended. His wife, Cecelia, supports them, he acknowledged, teaching health and nursing.

John says she will move anywhere he goes. He was proud to live in a working-class suburb, proud to have given up so many jobs. He was leaving in two days with their nine-year-old son for a month in Papua New

Guinea, hitching rides and catching boats.

But the tour he gave us of his home showed a real affection for his temporary posting. The town of Fremantle was a solid old port: stone buildings built with convict labor on narrow streets. And the pubs! Lots of pubs. It was easily the cleanest, most established port city of the dozens we'd seen. Nothing crumbling was in sight. All the facades sported new awnings.

Then I spotted the Perth headquarters of the Pacific & Orient company. The mighty P&O! Its ships opened up Australia to Asia, brought commerce and homesick colonials from Europe. The solid building reminded me of the short story "P&O" by Somerset Maugham I had just read in Singapore. Set in the 1920s, it was full of characters distanced from home, missionaries or expatriates working for rubber plantations, apart from families, growing psychologically isolated. Maugham's characters stayed away for years. Many never found a real home again. Today does airline travel make the expatriate life easier? Later I wondered what John might say about Maugham's restless characters and simultaneous yearnings for both adventure and home, and I wondered the same about myself.

He showed us the fish market, the beaches of Western Australia: yellow sand, wide almost as Rio de Janeiro's, and surging, tough surf. Every few miles along the beach were life-saving clubs with elaborate headquarters. I imagined being a life-saving club member could be the Perth equivalent of a volunteer fireman in Alabama or Tennessee. No pay but big social status.

We waded in the water, colder than the last beach I swam in on the Indian west coast at Kovalam. Slowly, John drove us back to Rob's house. We sat in the backyard and drank wine as the sun went down. How easy it all seemed! The weather was fine. These were new friends, with every chance of them being good friends. The conversation was simple and direct, particularly that with Rob and his wife, Sally. Rob is a native. Sally is from Melbourne.

He spoke haltingly, thinking before he talked. She had a terrific manner of holding your eye and smiling slowly. She said, "Uh-huh," while I talked, like women often to do to reassure you they're listening. We talked of Perth and the feeling it is distant, way out on the brink of the country. He is beginning a fancy research project in anesthesiology, something related to electricity.

They may want to move one day to our Cambridge, Massachusetts, or back to England where they lived for a year. His confidence seemed special. The strength of it may be based a lot on the lack of meaningful talk we've had with any other couples in months. But I believed anywhere they would be good friends.

CROSSING THE GREAT VICTORIA DESERT

THE ROAD FROM one side of Australia to the other is a new strip of asphalt across some of the oldest land on earth. It is not an easy drive.

The road builders grumbled, as they finished paving in 1967, that the sand contained a microorganism that ate asphalt. They were right. The surface looked as if the bugs had chewed it away from the edges toward the center stripe.

The famous way to cross this continent is the luxury train named the Indian Pacific. It's a glamorous Down-Under answer to the Orient Express. It would have made a delicious pairing with my Trans–Siberian trip. But the train workers were on strike. The Indian Pacific was not moving.

We could have taken a plane from west to east. But that didn't hold much challenge.

We decided the best way to cross Australia was sitting behind the driver of a commercial bus.

On a blistering day in February, in the middle of the Australian summer, Rob and I set out from Perth. The part in the driver's hair lined up with the center stripe. He told us stories about the desert and the people who live out here. He stopped to let me take pictures. The air-conditioning broke. We had a flat tire. By the time we reached the other side, 1,800 miles and two days later, I wondered why I'd never heard people talking about this trip. It is at once terrific and terrible.

The route retraced, backward, the path of Australia's early gold explorers. Just as in America, their search opened up the route for more settled settlers. But it was almost yesterday! The fabulous goldfields of Coolgardie and Kalgoorlie were not discovered until 1892, when somebody found a 125-pound nugget of pure gold just lying in the sand.

Coolgardie was a ghost town when we drove by. But Kalgoorlie hummed. We pulled into town at midnight, under a blaze of Christmas lights still hanging from the intersection. The streets were empty. I saw a quiet party sitting on the balcony of an old hotel. They were drinking in the dark, lighted by the decorations below.

The buildings haven't changed much since a young mining engineer named Herbert Hoover came to Kalgoorlie in 1897 straight from Stanford University. He loved it and gave his work in the Australian goldfields an energy that historians seldom credit him with in the US presidency.

The midnight partiers I saw were sitting atop the hotel where a love poem by the future US president hung in the lobby:

Did you ever dream, my sweetheart,
of a twilight long ago,
Of a park in old Kalgoorlie,
where the bougainvilleas grow,
Where the moonbeams on the pathways
trace a shimmering brocade,
And the overhanging peppers form
a lovers' promenade?

It's a saucy poem for the 1890s. Historians argue with the tale that he wrote it to a woman named Katherine, whom he did not marry. They argue whether he ever wrote it at all. The poem goes on:

And I spent my soul in kisses,
crushed upon your scarlet mouth,
Oh! My red-lipped, sun-browned sweetheart,
dark-eyed daughter of the south.

The poem stirred my interest in Hoover and the desert where he worked.

During his years there, construction began on a three-foot pipe to bring drinking water from the mountains near Perth across 350 miles of desert. That long silver pipeline paralleled the road. Out the bus window, I followed the pipeline with my eye, a shining thread quilting the mountains to the desert. When the pipe ended in Kalgoorlie, the desert seemed a lot closer.

And here, the bus driver discovered the air conditioner was broken. And worse, he could not repair it until Adelaide. We would cross the desert in midsummer, 110 degrees, just as those first gold seekers had. Sweating.

I fell asleep in my seat and at 5 a.m., the very darkest before the dawn part of the night, I woke up in Balladonia. It was a dry town with a dark history.

The center line of one of the world's straightest highways points east across the Nullarbor Plain.

A large rock marks the only water hole for hundreds of miles. It was here an Afghan camel driver arrived at sunset. The British settlers had brought Afghan workers and their camels to move supplies across the desert. But the British were clearly unwilling to accept the Afghan's Muslim traditions.

The driver was preparing for evening prayers by washing himself in the water. When the settlers rode up, they saw him with his feet in the only drinking water for hundreds of miles. They shot him dead in the back. In the trial that followed, they were acquitted.

Just outside Balladonia, I felt the bus bounce. The driver pulled off the road, and announced a flat tire. As he struggled to fix it, I explored the eucalyptus trees and saltbush by the side of the road. Silver green and spare, the leaves in the tops looked like suspended parachutes. The saltbushes make great sheep food, full of protein, but there aren't enough bushes to suit sheep farmers. Sheep stations here graze one sheep to 50 acres. Walking that far between mouthfuls makes the mutton pretty tough.

I would discover that tough mutton personally at lunch. Maybe the Australians shipped the tender cuts to the Middle East to help pay the country's fuel bill.

As the driver worked, I walked into the desert, smelling eucalyptus in the dark air. I felt the rock and sand underfoot. It was thin, and I sensed that my footprints would stay for years. Three billion years ago, these rocks formed when the earth itself barely held together. Little has changed since.

All day we drove across that bare crust of rock. All day the horizon kept holding my eyes. It was mesmerizing to see the sky meet the earth absolutely straight and clear. I had the sensation of driving through an early Mondrian painting—all grid, no curves.

That became the crucial test of those days, to survive and even enjoy the straight lines of road, sky, and desert. In the heat my eyes played tricks on me. The sand and the sky often switched places. A wedge-tailed eagle seemed to be swimming in the sand.

I tried to read some of Hemingway's short stories, which seemed as straightforward as the desert. But I couldn't concentrate. The pull of the desert view was too great.

We stopped for lunch at a poor restaurant in Madura called Restaurant. Evidently the economy of the desert extended to naming things, too. The waitress brought me a mutton pastry that had evidently missed the last boat to Saudi Arabia. She looked almost as tired as the food.

At each stop I tried to talk with the workers in the roadhouses, but nobody was in the mood. For normally chatty Australians, this was a serious discovery. Their faces were not at ease. The bar across the hall from the restaurant looked well worn. One man pulling a beer tap at one of the stops told me he never sees the same face twice.

At dusk the heat let go, and I dozed again in my seat. We passed Yalata, the mission town where white Australians tried to persuade native aborigines to settle. The collection of boomerangs and didgeridoos I saw there impressed me, but the housing looked like a dormitory from a church camp.

And then it was dark. Somewhere between the eucalyptus and the boomerangs, the bus slipped off the edge of the desert and onto fertile land. We had crossed the Great Victoria Desert. Low hills greeted us, green trees, curves. I even saw a harbor off to the right, where tuna boats were tied up to the dock at Ceduna.

Tuna. Ceduna. My mind tried to play with the rhyme, but I was too tired.

And at dawn we spotted the roofs of Adelaide. I was dreaming of a shower and a flat bed when we crossed the River Torrens.

There, below us under the bridge, was more water than the desert saw in literally a billion years.

I grabbed my Hemingway and suitcase and left the desert behind.

WONDERS DOWN UNDER

WOKE UP in Gladstone, Australia, at a $32-a-night B and B in a hammock for a bed. The second B in B and B was grilled fish and grilled tomatoes, then tea and Dramamine.

We caught the 8 a.m. cruiser out of Gladstone Harbor for Heron Island on the Great Barrier Reef.

The old green-turtle canning factory from 15 years ago is a thriving sea-turtle research institute now. But adding to our scant knowledge of the mysterious turtles turns out to be slow going. One scientist told me that learning turtle behavior from the only times humans see them as they lumber ashore to nest is like learning human behavior from only watching how women behave in a maternity ward.

That night I watched a green turtle mother toss waves of sand into the air 8 to 10 feet high, spraying my face. It is surprisingly noisy creating a nest for laying a clutch of eggs.

High tide at midnight. I knelt by 250 pounds or more of green-turtle flesh, her flippers more fishlike than reptile, her eyes weeping.

She dug down until the top of her back was below beach level, her smooth shell snowy with sand. The researchers reassured me she wasn't sad. These were not real tears, just salt-removal ducts. I was unconvinced.

Handfuls of hatchlings from previous nests crossed my path, hurrying to start life in the Coral Sea. I put one baby turtle in the pocket of my Himalayan Mountaineering Institute Windcheater, brought from Darjeeling, and walked with the last researcher to the water to let the turtle swim.

Days later we rode a New Zealand train pulling out of Auckland, New Zealand, past bony Norfolk pine trees. I was eager to see the South Island, with its famous walks and glaciers. But the train ride promised its own treats.

At 8:45 a.m., in the dining car, two young mothers with two children each were immediately served whiskeys. Outside the window a tall woman on a big horse raced the train, her sheepdog frisking alongside. I smiled at the memory of the Mongol horseman racing to meet the train in Siberia, on the other side of the world. It must be a universal truth that horses and trains attract each other.

By 1 p.m. I noticed that the train kept turning to the left. That was how I knew we'd begun to climb the fantastic engineering marvel called the Raurimu Spiral. In the universe of internationally unbelievable railroad rides, Raurimu may be the highest prize. As I pushed against the window for a better view, the mountain kept switching sides. We leaned into a horseshoe turn. Then another. And a third. Then the train made one complete loop around itself. We dived into two baby tunnels and passed a big ravine off to the right with waterfalls running into it. When we topped the plateau, we'd risen 700 feet in seven miles. The next stop, at a national park, did not include handing out Raurimu medals. Maybe one day they will create one, and I will come back to claim it. But I can dine out on the story in certain railroad circles for the rest of my life.

The South Island of New Zealand was a beautiful green and blue world, pierced with glassy glaciers and volcanic peaks like thorns. Beyond lay Antarctica. I was good for hiking those tongues of ice, but Antarctica was a little too far. We got only as close as the depot where boats sail for McMurdo Sound. The images of penguins, albatrosses, and stunning spare horizons contrasted with the settled steeples and town centers we'd seen in Christchurch.

To get across the South Island, we rented a car to drive one of the world's most frightening roads. It goes through the Haast Pass, near fjords, volcanoes, and glaciers. It was raining on a greasy slate road surface with steep sides. Big boulders sat uneasily on the verges. We crossed the Haast River on a new concrete-and-steel bridge. A little too new. The construction manager told me he intended to put the handrails up next week. The last flood months earlier had washed the bank away from the bridge. They'd now fastened chains on each of the ends so if the bank collapses again the bridge won't wash too far away.

It stopped raining by the time we descended to the river delta. The Haast River was broader here with little creeks joining in. Chelsea Creek would be a normal, babbling brook if the sun were out. Instead, it was gray. We did not talk much for the 15 miles or so it took the Haast to reach the Tasman Sea.

There was a tavern at the little town of Haast. I was ready for a warm room and cheerful faces after that drive. But no. The bar was huge. Chilly, and nobody smiled when we walked in.

They all wore lumberjack shirts. Foresting used to be big here, before national parks protected the mountainsides. Maybe 20 people sat under a sign carved on a wooden slab over the bar.

It read, "This is the last piece of wood milled in Haast before they shut down the people's livelihood to protect the forest." The sign ended with a warning: "If you are a conservation crank, don't boast about it in Haast."

After 20 cold minutes I couldn't stand sitting any more. We got up to leave. But a rough-looking woman at the door spoke to me.

"How d'ya like New Zealand?"

"Great, lovely," I said. "I bet Haast is nice when the sun shines."

"Well, it doesn't often."

I asked what does she do here?

"We are moss gatherers, all of us. Not many jobs around here now."

I wrinkled my forehead. She went on. "We dry the moss, and the Japanese buy it, to pack around their bulbs. Orchids they call them."

I asked where she finds the moss.

"In the swamp. We go into the swamp every day and gather moss." It was too much. I fled. The slippery road, the gray day, the chilly bar, and moss gathering in a swamp. I just wanted to get out of there.

On a ferryboat carrying people and cars across the turbulent waters
of the Marlborough Sounds, a cook takes a smoke break
with a journal-keeping traveler.

JOKES IN THE ANTIPODES

A SAILOR AND A PARROT are performing magic tricks on a boat during World War II. The parrot watches the rabbit disappear into the hat.

He tells the audience, "It's in the pocket, folks."

Then he watches a deck of cards disappear. "They're up the sleeve, folks."

Then a German submarine hits the ship. Everybody drowns except the sailor and the parrot. They drift for two weeks on a raft.

Finally, sunstruck, cracked, and dry, the parrot opens its beak. "Okay. I give up. What did you do with the ship?"

The water of the Marlborough Sounds is clear and blue, very deep in the long fingers of mildly salty water. I could be in the Maine woods here, or if the hills were a bit gentler, the mountains of east Tennessee. Geologists say the sounds are sunken riverbeds that reached the sea. And then, unlike most sounds, this entire north end tips into the Tasman Sea at a slant, as if trying to dislodge the North Island from underneath.

The result of that geologic struggle is a jagged coastline of unbelievable beauty. The soil is scratchy and thin. Second-growth pine trees are the only plantings that seem to hold. But they are thick and blue-green on the folds of the ridges, planted in rows like ribs.

An Englishman crash-landed in Africa. He's surprised to be greeted by a native speaking English. "May I *eooow eee owww* be of any assistance?"

"Well, you can tell me where you learned your language."

"That's easy. *Eeoow eeeow*. I picked it up from the shortwave."

The Abel Tasman track near the town of Motueka is a study in sudden contrasts. We hiked in and out of S curves along the very edge of the coast. Heading into the S, tall man-ferns edged the path. At the inmost corner, the noise of the surf quieted. Instead, we heard the softer sounds of a trickle or a torrent of water falling. Ferns. Moss. Water. Close, green and cool.

In minutes the outside of the S showed a breathtaking drop to the ocean. A bay with yellow sand and white mussel shells, scallops pink striped and flat. The air was clear. The trees were behind us ; instead of damp ferns the trail was edged in gorse and low bushes, sandy, well drained, no dirt. It was a world away from the previous 30 feet.

All afternoon, in and out, curling around the coast, a new angle on the bays and the surf at each turn.

Up at 5:45 a.m. for the early ferry from Picton back to the North Island. But it's a freight-only ferry, no room for us! I was trying to find the foreman to ask for a ride, when Jimmy the Cook found me. He was slightly tipsy, weaving a bit on his feet as he wheeled over and offered me galley passage.

Rob brought the bags up just as Jimmy the Cook was too sincerely into his offer to back out. One at a time boarding the boat, he whispered to us. First Jimmy walked me past the foreman, up the auto-loading ramp and into the galley. Then he took me straight to his room. This was feeling a bit sticky! He stashed my suitcase and poured three good fingers of vodka into a damp glass.

I was not sure he could find the door, let alone Rob. But we had 30 minutes until the ferry sailed. He assured me he would bring Rob back onto the boat with the morning newspapers and sat me in the galley to wait for the launch.

The crew seemed delighted at a new face. And with a cup of tea and a case of nerves I watched the clock. At 6:55 Jimmy—very red faced by now—brought the newspapers and Rob.

I was near the tipping point myself. Not with liquor but with our long-standing trip plan. Across the continents, no matter what, we were never to get on or off a boat, plane, or train without each other.

Rob arrived just in time for me not to have to make

a sudden exit. Good thing,

I might not have gotten off, it was so cozy in the galley. Warm, close, teacups and cutlery along the cabinets. The room was filled with long tables surrounded by hardworking men's faces looking at me with interest.

But Rob filled it even more. We laughed out loud at our good luck to make the ferry, congratulated ourselves on such fine traveling company in the galley, and felt the ferry move away from the dock.

Ron Baker, the chief cook's assistant (turned out Jimmy the Cook was the number-two potato-peeling assistant), joined in making us welcome. He told us hoary jokes that were a kind of time capsule. We had such fun I barely got up on deck in time to take a picture of the lighthouses on the eastern head of Wellington's bay.

Suva, Fiji, and Beyond

Dear Daddy,

I've been thinking of you all day as I wander through Suva, the capital of Fiji.

I wonder how it has changed since you steamed into the harbor with the US Army in 1943 from Noumea headed to the fighting for Bougainville in the Solomons.

I guess the hills are the same. I saw jagged mountains with sharp edges on top of each other. Blue all day with rain clouds. I guess that's the same too. It rained four times before noon.

Did you get off the ship and see the old colonial buildings? Five or six are still doing business on Victoria Parade. One is the home of the Suva Public Library. I went inside to find some pictures of this place when you were here.

A plump Indian woman in a sari tried to help me, but there wasn't much. Just one book of pictures of the entire South Pacific. I saw images of rusting cannons on beaches, barbed wire overgrown with orchids.

The library was pretty empty, so I left to find more people outside. I saw lots of Fijian men in long skirts. Their legs are muscled and strong and look good sticking out underneath. I remembered your telling me how you and your soldier friends snickered at the idea of Fijian soldiers in skirts… until you saw them in person.

One Fijian boat captain I talked to remembered the war well. He was a veteran himself. After the battle of Guadalcanal, when a boat full of New Zealand sailors was lost, he was sent in with other Fijians to replace them. He didn't want to recall too many details to me. He was tough looking, though. So I asked him about what I had read about Japanese prisoners of war on South Pacific islands. Japanese soldiers knew they faced rough treatment if arrested by Fijians. They'd walk half a day to surrender to a New Zealand, Aussie, or US soldier instead of the fierce Fijians. He nodded that was true.

I wandered through the market where they sell a hot milky tea in thick mugs. A bread man delivered loaves and stacked them like firewood on a rough counter. Beyond the market stood a warehouse curing coconut meat into copra. Thin crescents in square pails dried in the sun and smelled rich and oily. A trio of Fijians classing the copra told me they were getting it ready to ship to Australia to come back as margarine.

At 6:30 this morning I was one of the first people in the world to see the day begin. Pink clouds over the Suva harbor. It was not Mandalay, but yes, the sun came up like thunder. Yesterday I saw flying fishes play over the waves in Nadi harbor.

The Fiji Times was by my hand. "The first newspaper published in the World Today!" it boasts, because Suva is just west of the international dateline where the new day begins.

The wary gaze of skirt-wearing police officers
in Suva discourages rowdy behavior.

We flew in last night from Nadi in a furious rain-storm. Our Air Pacific 737 was full. But the Suva airport lacks jetways. We were going to have to scramble down wet steps. A handful of big black umbrellas waited at the cabin door. Five travelers grabbed them and scurried away to the lights of the terminal. Everyone else waited. A slickered attendant, a big, curly-haired Fijian in bright yellow rain gear ferried the umbrellas back. Five more passengers ran into the night. And again. And again.

Once we made it inside the terminal, I saw a low cabinet in the middle of the room. It held artifacts and an unbelievable record of Fiji's cannibal history. I was wide-eyed at the display of the carved wooden four-pronged forks used to eat people. The wood was dark, well oiled, and horrifying. The fork's very presence was a reminder that it was bad form to touch human flesh with your fingers while you were eating somebody else's human flesh.

Next to the fork was an odd-shaped artificial plant, with phony green leaves and fruit. A notice next to it called the plant a borodina.

It looked like a tomato shaped like an eggplant. A card said botanists had found it planted around Fijian temples, where it was used in ceremonies. They thought the cannibals made a sauce of the fruit and used the leaves as wrapping. I doubted much of this story, but there it sat, collecting frightened looks from every tourist on the plane.

Another card said the most notorious cannibal in Fijian history was a man named Ra Udrendre. Methodist missionaries said he claimed to have eaten almost 900 people: "872 stones in his tally line in 1849 as seen by Rev. R Blyth after Ra's death."

I was arrested by the display. Could not take my eyes off it. My simplest thought was this may not be the best way to greet international tourists.

Did you worry somebody wearing a skirt would eat you, Daddy? I'm getting homesick. See you soon.

LOVE, SALLY

The vast skies over the South Pacific hold airplanes full of eager tourists looking for the promise of adventure. On a night flight the captain summoned me to join the cockpit crew to watch us land. There was nothing to see beyond the glowing lights of the airplane controls lighting the pilots' faces from below. Through the radio I heard international air traffic controllers, their accents sounding like good old boys from Nashville, assuring us we were right on the track to descend. A speck of light glimmered in the window. It grew slowly. So much ocean. So little land.

Coconut meat pried from a dozen shells would
be used for oil, soaps, and cosmetics.

My cockpit adventure landing in Kathmandu had been daring because of the chance of crashing into the world's tallest mountains. This time the threat of missing the runway came from plunging into the waters of the deep blue Pacific ocean.

James Michener, in *Tales of the South Pacific*, wrote, "Polynesia's influence on world thought is far greater than its size would warrant. Musical names like Tahiti, Rarotonga, Bora Bora carry an emotional freight to all cold countries of the world, and Polynesia, the dying civilization, haunts the minds of white men who destroyed it."

In that cockpit, I wanted to find out if Michener was right, if the civilization was really dying at the hands of Westerners who cherished it as an escape. Our time on many islands in Tahiti and the Cook Islands would teach me what a vanilla plantation smells like, how to sleep on the deck of a heaving banana boat, how to pry a clam from the reef and eat it raw.

The light grew in front of the plane, summoning us like a deer caught in the headlights of a hunter's pickup truck. The pilots glanced up at my stare and smiled. Perhaps they invited me because they wanted to share the experience with someone new or simply were bored with each other. I didn't care. I was the deer. I couldn't take my eyes off that beam of light pulling us down to a tiny airstrip on a magical island.

FISH OF ANOTHER REEF
ALWAYS GO BACK TO
THEIR REEF

RAROTONGA, the Cook Islands. A ukulele plays. Hibiscus blooms. In the air the sweet perfume of frangipani blends unforgettably with the sharp odor of spider conch shells drying on the porch.

Radio Rarotonga plays Mickey Gilley's "Talk to Me."

It was Friday night at the Banana Court Bar. A Hawaiian named Dick told me he's building a fruit-drying factory on nearby Atiu. It is a tiny little island, where Dick flew in a Sabena he rented for $40,000 a month to collect dried pineapple to sell to health-food stores across the United States.

I was learning the finer points of pineapple drying when Dick looked down the bar and recognized somebody. They smiled at each other. Dick lowered his voice and told me the big slack-jawed man with light hair and a goofy smile was the son of Sir Albert Henry, the prime minister of the Cook Islands.

While he whispered, the man came straight to our table. I expected an introduction, but instead the man stuck a bare foot under my chair and fished out the flip-flop he'd left behind.

Later we were sitting at a low table when Elvis started singing "Blue Suede Shoes." Another bar guest asked me to dance. He was a Radio New Zealand political correspondent named Trevor Henry. He turned out to be a better talker than dancer.

He confirmed the identity of the flip-flop finder: the son of the man who had led the Cook Islands to independence from New Zealand. Albert Henry had been knighted by Queen Elizabeth in 1974 at the end of the airport we'd flown into days before. It was a ceremony imaginable only in the South Pacific, in a hut swaddled in coconut palm branches.

Sir Albert Henry ran things for a while. But other islanders eventually resented his patronage ways. They got together and had voters in New Zealand buy airplane tickets to fly back to the islands to vote against him.

So Sir Henry got some Cook Island dollars together and chartered six airplanes full of voters in Auckland to even things up. The dollars came from an American helping organize the Cook Island Philatelic Bureau. (Stamps are big business in the Cooks. New issues make up a big chunk of the island's budget.)

Then the courts heard a case against Sir Henry, who was charged with using public stamp money to influence votes. They found him guilty. And for the first time in history a court created by a democracy replaced one government with another one. So said Trevor Henry.

I looked this up, and it's true.

Then the American stamp promoter was prosecuted in the United States under the new "Lockheed" antiforeign corruption statutes. The first successful prosecution ever. Or so said Trevor Henry of Radio New Zealand. Not so sure if this is true.

But it *is* true that the Queen un-knighted Sir Henry. He died a mister, not a sir.

It might not have been such a happy family by the time he died.

That man I had just seen, who fished his flip-flop from under my chair? This was clearly not the first time he'd been spending a Friday night in the Banana Court Bar. Even Sir Henry knew his son did not have what it took to lead the nation. Before he died, the former prime minister put up his nephew as opposition leader instead.

A few days later, I left the harbor in Avarua, Rarotonga, for the outer island of Aitutaki, 140 miles away. Aboard the *Mataora*, a banana boat registered in the Kingdom of Tonga in the town of Nuku'alofa. Like Michener, I was captured by these names with their singing vowels. I said them over and over. Diesel engines pulled the boat from the harbor in a sprinkling rain. A great wave pointed the bow into the sky. We came down like a roller coaster.

The heaving deck of a freighter is a temporary home for passengers sleeping underneath a tented tarp. Freight-shipping vessels like the *Mataora* gave Cook Islanders the chance to island-hop and visit relatives throughout the South Pacific.

I found a seat in the galley as the boat slid sideways. I opened my Cook Island library copy of *Moby Dick* and started to read. "Call me Ishmael…Having little or no money in my purse… I thought I would sail about a little and see the watery part of the world."

Soon the watery part of my world was getting a little more rollicking than I liked. I needed to see the horizon to settle my stomach. I went up onto the deck. Stretching beyond me on top of the cargo of stoves and boilers and beer were a dozen people using the boat as a ferry service. Some were flat on their backs on the deck since we'd left Avarua, saying they wouldn't lift their heads until Aitutaki was in sight. Seasickness, they said.

Suddenly I couldn't enjoy the view any longer. I hurtled to the rail and threw up everything I'd eaten the day before.

This was a solo trip for me. I wanted a break from Rob, a couple of days exploring a new island, and I might have been nervous. Or perhaps it was the cheese-bacon-flavored corn curls from the snack bar at the Avarua harbor.

In 30 seconds I felt wonderful. The pink sky was gorgeous. The air on the open deck felt better than my cabin below. I lay down beneath the tarp and fell asleep. At midnight I woke up and made my way between the sleeping bodies of fellow passengers to stand at the bow. The moon was full, directly overhead. All the water around me was bright and clear. I saw a dozen flying fishes sailing from one wave to another. A wave broke 50 feet away, its crest glittering in the moonlight. The wind was warm. The next wave broke over my feet. I took a long, deep breath of salty air and went back to sleep. At 6:30 the sun woke me up as it dawned off to the right. Solid sleep, no twinge of nausea. I thought maybe that was the last time I would ever be sick.

EASTER WITH THE COOKS

O N PALM SUNDAY the Titikaveka Christian Church filled rapidly. High white walls, brown painted pews, and narrow clear-glass windows held an energetic crowd of Cook Islanders. I climbed the worn concrete steps to the balcony and sat with teenage boys peering over the side rail making faces at each other. Their feet were bare and dusty from a long drought that had been holding the Cook Islands dry for weeks.

Slowly I realized this half of the balcony was the boys' side. I turned to the beefy 17-year-old next to me and asked him if I should move. He nodded silently and looked very relieved as I scooted away on the opening organ chords. The girls' side had a lot more babies and giggles.

From the corner during the prayer I counted the crowd below. Two hundred forty-five people, with another hundred on each side of me in the balcony. That is 445 people, none of them still. All the women below me wore broad-brimmed straw hats. The men wore short sleeves and long trousers. And they all sang. Oh, did they sing.

The music started as I arrived. Walking up I heard big sounds. I thought it was choir practice for the thunderous parts of Handel's *Messiah*. But no. The congregation was just killing time till ten o'clock. One heavyweight singer in the back led from her pew. She wore an orange hat with a blue ribbon and sang with a strong voice, pure as gold. She sang three or four notes and without anybody so much as turning around. the congregation jumped in precisely together.

How can I tell you what it sounded like? It was rich as the spirituals in the Abyssinian Baptist Church in Holly Springs, Mississippi. But the notes were sharp, with clear attacks, lots of fast precision, like cavalry calls. And they were thick with harmonies. I counted seven or eight choices of notes per chord. I had never heard singing like it. The organ seemed totally unnecessary. After its opening chords marked the end of the warm-up and the beginning of the service, I did not hear the organ again.

The sermon began with a wave of hands from the preacher and a flourish of eyebrows. That's about all I understood. The church bulletin listed an English order of service with hymns in Maori. The pastor let us know he was preaching on Jesus' triumphal entrance into Jerusalem. His voice rose and fell hypnotically.

After a few minutes I slipped outside and found another hundred people waiting. Talking, feeding babies, sitting on the edges of the graves that surrounded the big church. Some new gravestones held vivid photographs of the deceased in ceramic ovals.

Then I heard the sermon winding down. I stepped

back into the vestibule just as the churchgoers were starting to sing the only tune I recognized, Number 69: "Immortal, Invisible, God Only Wise."

The preacher walked down the aisle wearing a black robe over his wine-colored suit. He shook hands inside and out. The churchyard filled with waves of Cook Islanders. Ladies in those big hats greeted each other, swooping in beneath the brims for gentle pecks on the cheek with the practiced precision of fighter pilots. Children collected their parents, couples cranked their Honda cycles, and church was over.

A week later, it was Easter Sunday. This time the preacher switched languages sentence by sentence. We sang "Jesus Christ Is Risen Today" in Maori. I hummed along until we got to the Alleluias. The minister's last words, his benediction, was a plea for rain. "Send us rain!" he prayed. "Fill our water tanks, oh, Lord!"

A big tea at the manse across the road followed the service. Banana cakes, papayas, mackerel sandwiches, buttered cabin bread with green tomato slices. I asked a matron in a white dress and hat why such an elaborate spread? She said everyone was supposed to bring a plate, but last week everyone forgot. They had only one plate of biscuits. So this week everyone remembered. It was a great sacrifice, given the cost of vegetables since the drought here.

After midnight it began to rain and kept up until morning.

So Many Islands.
So Many Vowels!

AN ELDERLY CHINESE boat captain made two big circles a day, wearing blue jeans and flip-flops as he steered his flat-end barge inside the reef protecting Raiatea and Taha'a. He let Rob and me squeeze in between gasoline drums and watermelon, Portland cement and corned beef. The break in the sandbar outside Raiatea was narrow. We went fast across the deep blue lagoon to the other island, Taha'a. The barge motored clockwise all the way around it, touching at eight villages hidden under a canopy of coconut palms. Above the smell of the outboard motor I caught the scent of vanilla plantations. *Vanilla tahitensis.*

The docks were coral and concrete blocks, stretching a few feet away from the bays into absolutely clear water. Sometimes we saw beaches of peach or yellow sand, thick grained and clean. Sometimes the green leaves and branches came right to the edge of the blue water. Here a white canoe outrigger was pulled up between pandanus roots, a speargun resting inside. These islands are high in the middle with bony ridges poking straight out and down, like the outline of a hand stretched out and up on its fingertips. The people live in the flat webs between the fingers in low, one-story houses. And I counted six corrugated roofs for every remaining thatched roof. They rusted red and handsome under the green mountain above. At Tapuamu, the boat driver delivered a 100-pound valve. Then a bicycle. And then the driver himself. He peddled off and in five minutes came back with a Coca-Cola.

In the distance the blue tooth of Bora-Bora prodded the sky.

We had flown into Tahiti's capital, Papeete, near midnight a few days before. All the hotels were full, so we settled in at the bar to stay up all night for the 6 a.m. flight to the island of Bora-Bora. As the sun came up, our little plane cleared the runway.

Half an hour later we landed first on the island of Huahine. Ten air minutes later, Raiatea, a bigger airport on a bigger volcanic island. And 10 more minutes to the jagged peak of Bora-Bora. But we couldn't simply taxi to the main town, Vaitape. We left the airstrip on a sandy atoll, piled into a launch, and boated for 20 more minutes to the dock in Vaitape.

Here, finally, a 10-minute walk on foot from the dock was our pension, Chez Amie, where $14 US dollars bought us a room. By now I was stumbling from the overnight in Papeete's international airport bar. But the day was young.

So we walked back to town to explore. Everything seemed to be in slow motion inside the reef edge of tiny outer islands called *motus*. We watched the Oa Oa Yacht Club get a new roof of palm leaves after two recent cyclones. In slow motion ourselves, we made only two promises for the day: to circumnavigate the 30 miles around Bora-Bora and to snorkel in the lagoon by the fancy Bora-Bora Hotel. ($150/night. No thanks, no vacancy anyway.)

The French motorbike known as a *motobécane* was a challenge. It was fun to pronounce the name and cost $18 for two for two hours. The rental shop told me you have to pedal fast to start it.

I was terrified. Hot oil popped out on my toes and ankles as we rode. It took an hour, halfway around the island, before I was comfortable. But every 20 feet traveled gave me a new angle on the mountain looming above us. The village edge gave way to single houses, plain and mostly open to the air. Many were painted turquoise. All had laundry on clotheslines, and each line held at least one pareu, a garment that floated in stunning pastel colors: soft coral and green and blue, the shades waving into each other.

I realized that if I was out of sorts, sleepy, grumpy with an oil-burned ankle, I could simply go on making myself miserable or I could get over it. I gave myself the rest of the trip around the island to decide. That's when I spotted the snorkel rental at the fancy Bora-Bora Hotel, and I was over it.

Underwater in the lagoon the coral was drab but

the fish brilliant. The clear water allowed a deep view. I was able to watch the fish chase each other around. In Fiji for the first time I had heard parrot fish chomping on coral. It sounded like a busy barber shop: snip, chomp, click. There I saw spiny urchins, ferny corals, nudibranchs, in yellow, pink, and blue. I even followed a manta ray through the water. It floated like a bird, with a surprising bird face. Here, in Tahiti, fishes little and big left clouds of coral mud behind as they darted. Schools of a tan-and-black fish were new to me. Too quickly we shook off the salt water to return the treacherous *motobécanes*.

That night, over rum and Coke, we had dinner with archaeologist Lindsey Sharman, an Australian living under a fig tree on Bora-Bora. He said he was only interested in people once they were dead, which his avid conversational skills proved to be untrue. Lindsey does fieldwork for a seismologic oil-exploration company out of Houston and, in fact, he really did live under a fig tree.

We sat down at the outside table in the sand by an open-air restaurant full of men who'd been drinking since noon. I ordered plates of the fish special and listened to Lindsay hold forth on a fascinating unraveling of the gene pools of Australoids, Melanesians, and the future strength of the hunter-gatherers. His main point seemed to be that the gene pool for the world after The Bomb will not be the genes of us from the West but the people least likely to be the bomb targets, the Africans and native Australians, who will carry on exactly as they do now.

He seemed delighted to share a new theory of island population origins. The genes of the Maoris on New Zealand, he said, prove they migrated there from these very islands. From neighboring Raiatéa in A.D. 900 to 1200 their canoes left through a break in the reef for New Zealand. Lindsay's theory is the islanders who left Raiatea were too hotheaded to stay in peaceful Polynesia. He says they were the Che Guevaras, the rebels who left first, perhaps because they lost a battle with the more pacifist Raiateans. The society they set up in New Zealand is more warlike, more structured, more aggressive than the society they left, he concluded.

His harangue was interrupted by a large bang. The noise level in the restaurant escalated. A beer bottle found its way to a man's face. Not so pacifist at the moment.

Quickly we dived around the trunk of a palm tree. The fight boiled up and over, and one of the big hunter-gatherers was pulled into the road to slug it out with another man. It took 10 minutes to settle down. Somehow, it felt very familiar. I had covered fights like this in tough spots like Orange Mound, near Memphis, or at Libs Café, on the road to Calera, Alabama. Places where people go to drink and fight must be universal. Maybe the gene pool surviving The Bomb will be more diverse than Lindsey thought.

Quietly I asked again for the fish. Soon carefully arranged plates of raw mahi-mahi arrived, with tomatoes, onions, and salt. Slabs of French bread and butter. A perfect supper. We paid Fr.800, six dollars, and walked to Chez Amie.

COCONUT CREAM
IN MY COFFEE

LAST NIGHT WE cracked open a dry coconut. Our goal was coconut oil, squeezed from the very coconut palms we'd seen growing that day. We borrowed an electric grater and soon filled a bowl with fluffy grated coconut.

But I wanted coconut oil, not fluff. I wanted to taste coconut cream in a cup of coffee. I didn't know how to strain the grated coconut at first. There were no clean towels or kitchen cloths in sight.

But in my suitcase was an orange bandanna. It had saved my neck from sunburn in India, held back my hair hiking in the Himalayas. Best of all, it was clean. So I filled it with the coconut fluff and start squeezing.

The coconut oil spurted white through my fingers. I gave it a good squeeze and was rewarded with a gentle trickle into a bowl.

Then Shelly Cinnamon, a fellow traveler we'd met on the island, took over, milking the orange bandanna. At her last squeeze, the fabric parted. She was horrified.

But to me it was a sign.

My wardrobe was telling me it was time to go home.

Days later, flying east, I saw California's Catalina Island first, off the left side of the plane bringing us back to the United States. Catalina looked more worn than Tahiti, steeper than the Cook Islands, darker than Fiji. The sun was setting out there in the Pacific. It caught me full in the eyes. I was crying a little. I was glad to be home.

When I get home, I will have a lot to tell. But will I have anything to say?

EPILOGUE

"As a traveller, Ibn Battutah was by no means unique. The difference was that he wrote his travels down..."

TIM MACKINTOSH-SMITH, *editor,*
The Travels of Ibn Battutah

ONE OF THE WORLD'S greatest travelers was a fabulous Islamic writer. In Nepal I had read Marco Polo's stories of the Silk Road to China. Years later I discovered Marco Polo's contemporary, a chattier storyteller from Morocco named Ibn Battuta. He covered a broader swath of the globe in the 1300s and ran into people from home everywhere he went.

His modern translator, Tim Mackintosh-Smith, reminds us we know Ibn Battuta and his adventures not because of the places he went but through the stories he told.

Home was all I'd missed and more. I caught up on family with a visit in Denver to Great Aunt Jule. A stop in Lincoln, Nebraska, to see my grandmother Perdita, Aunt Joan, and Cousin Billy. Stories of my great adventure poured out of me at first. Then they trickled and slowly stopped.

Life began all over again. Rob went home to Memphis. I took a new TV job in Dallas and then Atlanta. A package the size of a Smithfield ham arrived from the Carpet Factory at Darjeeling's Tibetan Self-Help Refugee Centre. It showed Siberian cranes mating for life on a bed of blue wool sky.

Rob and I did not mate for life. Not from lack of my trying for a year or more. I grew increasingly impatient as he postponed a decision on marriage. Finally I gave up waiting. A year later a newsroom colleague caught my eye. Tall, good looking, and the father of two beautiful girls. We married in 1988. Our baby, Will, arrived in 1991.

Rob kept traveling. He wrote a 500-page book called *The Traveler's Tool Kit* and included a photo from our time in Ladakh. He moved to Canada for much of the year and wrote award-winning fiction. His heroes sounded like him: single, moving easily around the world with good-looking women, settling international mayhem. Years later, when I looked for that jade ring from Thailand I could not find it.

The world had changed while I was gone, and I had, too. I was not done with traveling. But my restless need for new places and people yielded to a desire to set down roots. All the lessons from my year away taught me it was time to listen to Voltaire's Candide, to find and tend my own garden.

Every news story dug me deeper into the lives of people who make the news. Many times I met them at the worst moment of their lives. Often they shared with me how they got there. How the car broke, or the husband had a girlfriend, or the baby died, and the pain was too great to bear without leaning on drugs or alcohol.

I covered the wrecked remainders of the Jim Crow South. Many stories in the proud Civil Rights city of Atlanta showed how much was left to be done to meet the promises of racial equality. Drugs sucked the soul away. Democrats gave way to Republican politicians, but party changes made little difference in state policies toward poorer Georgians.

Atlanta's growth began to seem a long way away from the rest of Georgia. When new reporters arrived from smaller markets around the country, I chuckled as they realized Atlanta was actually in a very different place called Georgia.

As the century turned, I told more stories about the dynamic growth of Atlanta.

I paddled the Chattahoochee River and saw sewer systems neglected for decades harm the beautiful waters we depended on for drinking.

I drove the sprawling suburbs where I could see the tension between miserable commutes and desires for a bigger house and yard.

When Will was 10, I stopped covering daily news, concentrating on special longer stories about the costs and rewards of growth.

I helped college roommate Eileen begin a public

charter school in an underserved part of town. It quickly outdistanced the academic outcomes of the neighborhood schools.

Slowly the world beyond news grew more important to me. I joined the board of an organization restoring a park designed by Frederic Law Olmsted. Voltaire's suggestion of tending my own garden was taking root.

But I never stopped turning over stories in my head from those travels.

I realized how often the people I had met traveling were unhappy with where they lived.

Expatriates, college professors, restaurateurs in the desert spent a lot of energy wishing they were elsewhere. Perhaps I found them then because I was searching for my place in the world. I did not see that restlessness again until the pandemic kept us all from traveling.

When the coronavirus stopped the world, the passenger flights from Hartsfield-Jackson Atlanta International Airport disappeared from the sky overhead, and all my travel plans disappeared as well. When would I be able to go to see the sand-hill-crane migrations in Grand Island, Nebraska? I wondered. Would I ever take that barge up the Rhone? Would Johannesburg stay unexplored? I despaired that the fun of visiting new places would be gone for a long time. I worried that I would not stay invigorated without the ease of nonstop flights to faraway places now made sophisticated by waves of modern travelers. But these thoughts faded as the weeks wore on, and COVID tests and infection rates claimed my attention.

Then in a fit of pandemic-escape basement cleaning I found a box of travel souvenirs: a handful of South Pacific seashells. A curious clutch of lapel pins in Chinese and Russian alphabets. Journals full of people and places encountered in the very farthest corners of the world in 1982 and 1983.

As I read them, I realized how different my traveling habits had become. I don't keep journals anymore. My aerogram letters to family on thin blue paper have been swapped for social-media pictures and captions. Travel may be faster and easier, but it is missing something important. And I began to wonder if this disconnect, this COVID-forced pause in travel, might yield a fresh look at what it means to travel with more care and to reconsider what stays alive after a journey.

I could never repeat the travel adventures of the 1980s. Today I'd never make it to the cockpits of airplanes. Bicycles in Beijing wouldn't require a passport. Mao and Lenin may still look the same in eternal repose, but I would not bet on either one.

I *could* take that Trans-Siberian train again to see if China-Russia tensions are still alive. The Russian Railroad says it offers twice a day service from Moscow to Beijing. It costs $675.92 according to the official website. But the page crashed when I checked for a reservation.

When North Korea barged into the headlines, I thought of my interrogation by the women's basketball team chaperones on the train in Siberia. Their complaints have likely not changed.

The Baikul-Amur Railway is finished. A website touts it as an intrepid trip, an overlooked gem on tracks supposedly completed two years after I met the steel-toothed worker at breakfast. Russian travel writers, however, acknowledge that the construction continued until 1991.

When Pakistani troops stoned Indian soldiers to death in 2020, I knew those hostilities I saw from the airport in Ladakh are still the same.

Some things have changed, and for the better.

That great one-horned rhino we hunted on elephant back? Conservation efforts on the Nepali-Indian border are saving it from extinction. The population has grown over the 40 years from those 200 lumbering giants then to more than 3,500.

A happy recording surfaced on the internet in the spring of 2020. I peered at a bright blue sea foaming with what looked like white confetti. A reporter's voice said a drone camera did what thousands of volunteers could not do: provide a more accurate count of the green turtles swimming to nest on the islands of the Great Barrier Reef. Each of those confetti dots was a turtle aiming for the place where she was born.

Sea-level counters had underestimated the turtles' population by 50 percent. Despite the oceans' harm from climate change and plastic garbage, those green turtles I watched weeping as they laid their eggs are in better shape than we thought.

The years since I set out to see the world, now four decades ago, have settled me, like the turtles, close to where I was born. Yet my travels with family and friends since that trip keep my passion for new places alive.

Philosopher Alain de Botton in his *Art of Travel* says journeys are the midwives of thought. I think he is right. The thoughts from those travels helped form a person deeper, richer, slower. The baby my journey delivered is older now, yet I would get back on that road again to see what is out there now. But someday. Not tomorrow. For now, I have so many stories to share of the here and now. There is so much good work to be done at home.

And when it's time to travel again, I hope to capture the joys of it as carefully as I once did.

Memphis Commercial Appeal photographer Fred Griffith captured
friends at the WMC assignment desk in January 1981.
Left to right: Sally Sears, Pat Neal, Susan Jerkins,
Nancy Hart, and (front) Janet Morris.

ACKNOWLEDGMENTS

Thanks to my Memphis colleagues at WMC Television who endured my travel planning in early 1982. News leaders Frank Gardner and Jim Zarchin, Borys Tomaszczuk, Russell Ruffin, anchor Mason Granger, and a station full of friends listened and smiled.

The company and advice Rob Sangster shared so generously on the road and in the years since are an enduring part of my life.

Steve Sears made the traveling finances easier for those penniless days of the trip. He kept accounts, transferred money from one bank to another, and even sprinted to Montevallo's Merchants and Planters Bank to cover a personal check somehow cashed for me in Singapore. Randie Sears Rosenberg made herself a lively, frequent audience applauding for years at the telling and retelling of these stories. They remain constant believers in the joys of family and travel.

Jonny Hines, Ellen Porter, and Eileen Harvey Bakke helped me find fascinating connections with Princetonians around the world.

Pam Brown Phagan listened with the heart of a childhood best friend.

The enthusiasm of Rutledge Forney filled dips along the trail.

Jeannine Addams, Amy Cromwell, and Becky Evans encouraged a wider sharing of these adventures.

Joan Tapper knows the best adventure travel writing and writers. She found some here she thought worth sharing, and I'm grateful she did.

John Balkwill coaxed the manuscript into a beautiful book with the care and high quality he began to practice in Tuscaloosa at the University of Alabama's Institute for the Book Arts.

For Richard and Will, I regret the writing time that cost me your company. I hope you think this book is worth it. Sharing stories about our travels together makes the world a more interesting place. I'm ready to go somewhere with you right now.

ABOUT THE AUTHOR

SALLY SEARS is an award-winning news reporter and environmentalist. She is a native of Montevallo, Alabama, and a magna cum laude graduate of Princeton University. She lives in Atlanta with her husband, Richard.